THE GUERRILLA GUIDE TO
CREDIT REPAIR

2ND EDITION

ALSO BY TODD BIERMAN

The Fix Your Credit Workbook
(with David Masten)

THE GUERRILLA GUIDE TO
CREDIT REPAIR

2ND EDITION

HOW TO FIND OUT WHAT'S WRONG WITH YOUR CREDIT RATING—AND HOW TO FIX IT

TODD BIERMAN AND NATHANIEL WICE

REVISED AND UPDATED BY
ANDREA COOMBES

ST. MARTIN'S GRIFFIN ☙ NEW YORK

Note to the Reader

The information presented in this book is intended as a general guide to assist consumers in improving their credit rating. As different consumers have different credit histories, results from employing the methods in this book may vary. Neither this nor any other book should be used as a substitute for professional legal advice.

Also, the authors recommend several Web sites and other resources where readers may find additional and updated information on various topics. However, bear in mind that neither the publisher nor the authors have control over, or responsibility for, the content of these resources or, in the case of Web sites, the policies of their providers. Likewise, reference in this book to these resources as potential sources of additional information does not mean that either the authors or publisher endorse anything that might be said there.

THE GUERRILLA GUIDE TO CREDIT REPAIR, 2ND EDITION. Copyright © 2006 by Todd Bierman and Nathaniel Wice. All rights reserved. Printed in the United States of America. No part of this book may be used or reproduced in any manner whatsoever without written permission except in the case of brief quotations embodied in critical articles or reviews. For information, address St. Martin's Press, 175 Fifth Avenue, New York, N.Y. 10010.

www.stmartins.com

Library of Congress Cataloging-in-Publication Data

Bierman, Todd.
　　The guerrilla guide to credit repair : how to find what's wrong with your credit rating—and how to fit it / Todd Bierman and Nathaniel Wice ; revised and updated by Andrea Coombes.—2nd ed.
　　　　p. cm.
　　ISBN 0-312-34025-7
　　EAN 978-0-312-34025-4
　　1. Consumer credit—United States. I. Wice, Nathaniel. II. Coombes, Andrea. III. Title.

HG3756.U54B5 2006
332.7'43—dc22　　　　　　　　　　　　　　　　　　　　　　2005044604

First Edition: January 2006

10 9 8 7 6 5 4 3 2 1

Contents

INTRODUCTION

Overview of credit reporting

If you ever wondered whether a permanent record would follow you throughout your life, the answer these days is a definitive yes. And if the Information Age has given birth to Big Brother, it's the credit-reporting industry.

Nearly every adult in America is tracked by three main corporations—TransUnion, Experian, and Equifax—which together generate more than 1 billion credit reports each year, most of them bought by creditors, employers, and insurers.

Even though credit reporting has evolved into a multibillion-dollar business, only recently has it received much public scrutiny. No one these days should be surprised to learn that this largely unsupervised system can be grossly erratic and unfair.

Credit reports are the lifeblood of our credit-driven economy. When you apply for a loan—whether it's a credit card, a mortgage, or for a car or college—and sometimes even for a job, insurance, or an apartment rental, someone is going to check your credit report. A credit report can clear or disqualify your application or, more insidiously, determine the terms of acceptance, such as the interest rate on a loan (higher and thus more expensive for someone with a spotty report). It's estimated that each of the three main agencies collects more than 2 billion pieces of information each month, and, based on that information, lenders pronounce citizens creditworthy or not.

The detail and scope of information in the bureaus' computer credit reports can be shockingly personal and surprisingly public. Almost anyone who wants your report can get it. More ominous still, credit reports are often filled with errors. Some studies estimate that as many as one-quarter of credit reports have mistakes that would hamper a consumer's access to credit. It's common, for instance, for the credit bureaus to mix up the separate credit histories of two people with the same name.

The credit-reporting system can be confusing and intimidating, especially for people who have gotten into credit trouble. No creditor can push you around or harass you once you've read our credit book. Following simple instructions, you can manage what the credit bureaus say about you. This book won't get you out of your debts, but it will help you change the way they are reported.

Even consumers who've never paid a bill late may find they have credit problems: Identity theft and the fraud that goes with it are a growing cause of credit-report errors.

A 2003 Federal Trade Commission report estimated that almost 10 million people have been victims of some form of identity theft, losing a total of $5 billion. Meanwhile, the cost to financial services companies and other businesses totaled almost $50 billion.

The steep cost of identity theft and its growing prevalence have prompted greater scrutiny of what was for years a largely unregulated credit-reporting industry. Recent laws have led to greater transparency about how the system works, and thus greater protections, but consumers are still low on the totem pole. In this industry, the credit bureaus' customers are lenders and other creditors, and that means consumers must still fight for their rights.

How does this book work?

Even if your credit is good, so much is riding on your credit history that it's in your interest to regularly check your credit report and clear any mistakes or other damaging information.

This book is organized into three main steps to clear your credit:

- Get your credit report
- Read your credit report
- Repair your credit report

You can set the repair process in motion today by requesting copies of your credit reports from each of the three main bureaus. If you already know which account history you want to dispute (a credit card, a car loan, etc.), you can begin the process immediately.

How does credit repair work?

This book raises a question: Can the average citizen really change what credit bureaus report? The answer is yes. It's not always easy, but more often than not the credit-reporting system rewards consumers who are persistent.

The secret of credit repair has a simple logic. Even though they may act like it, credit bureaus are not God or government. Under current law, their right to mind other people's business—to sell information about you—comes with the responsibility to substantiate the information if it's challenged.

Credit repair is the process of persistently challenging the credit bureaus to document their information. The credit bureaus are expert at ignoring these challenges for technical reasons, but the system ultimately favors the persistent consumer who navigates the labyrinthine process. Why? Because, incredibly, the credit bureaus and creditors are so sloppy at verifying their information that they often prefer to restore your credit rather than to prove that it's bad. When you exercise your rights, you turn the unfairness of the credit-reporting system against itself. The credit bureaus convict without proof, but when pressed, they also exonerate without proof.

Credit bureaus aren't always the source of the problem. Creditors, who report to the credit bureaus, can be negotiated with and convinced to stop saying bad things about you. The **advanced** section walks you through creditor negotiations. Although most lenders value your patronage, the firm exercise of your rights under consumer laws is what usually persuades the creditor to clear your name.

THE CREDIT-REPAIR INDUSTRY

The credit-repair industry operates at the fringes of other businesses. The size of the industry is difficult to measure, in part, because credit-repair efforts are, by design, invisible to the credit bureaus.

But the credit-repair industry has more than its fair share of quacks. One standard ruse is to promise a new "credit identity." After you pay a hefty upfront fee, you're advised to apply for an employer identification number to use instead of your Social Security number when applying for credit, but it's a federal crime to make false statements on a credit application and to misrepresent your Social Security number.

There have been so many complaints of unfulfilled promises and outright consumer rip-offs that Congress passed the Credit Repair Organizations Act in 1996, which forbids credit-repair companies from asking for payment before services have been rendered, among other requirements. See Appendix IX for the text of the Act.

Credit-repair scams may have made it harder for consumers to fight credit errors on their own. Some experts say credit-repair ruses—such as bombarding the credit-reporting agencies (CRAs) with so many dispute letters that the CRAs can't respond within the mandated time period—have increased the likelihood of CRAs flagging disputes as frivolous and not responding to them. Thus, it's important, when corresponding with the CRAs, to use your own words, and to base your claims on the consumer laws that are designed to protect you.

We hope that our book will empower consumers at a fraction of the upwards of $500 that credit-repair services often charge. As the Federal Trade Commission says in an online consumer guide: "Everything a credit repair clinic can do for you legally, you can do for yourself at little or no cost."

Even with our book, there's still a place for the experienced credit practitioner, especially in the area of legal issues, like filing court motions. Part of being educated about what you can do is knowing what you can't do. *The Guerrilla Guide* also teaches how to find and use a lawyer. Even then, this book is essential reading for working with a credit counselor or lawyer.

You won't always need a lawyer, but the credit dispute process definitely requires patience and persistence. One problem that sometimes arises is that erroneous information the consumer has successfully removed from the report winds its way back on there again when the furnisher starts re-reporting the information.

Another difficulty you might face is that the report your potential lender pulls using partial information about you, such as just your name and Social Security number, may be a "mixed" or "subfile," which combines your information with that of another consumer with a similar name or Social Security number. When you get denied credit based on this mixed file, and request your report from the reporting agency to see what the problem is, the report you receive after providing your more complete identifying information, including recent addresses and other identifiers, won't have that same erroneous data, and will leave you stumped as to why you were denied credit. In cases such as this, consumers must be persistent, working with both the reporting agencies and creditors, and possibly hiring an attorney as well.

No matter what the state of your credit at this point, remember that consistently paying your bills on time is the most direct route to a squeaky-clean credit report. When extending credit, lenders focus on your recent actions more than on past problems. The same is true with most credit score models: Late payments within the past few years will count against you more than old bad accounts. Even as you dispute errors on your reports, make sure you pay your current bills on time.

GET YOUR CREDIT REPORT

Introduction

Getting your credit reports is the first step to challenging their contents. In years past, the credit bureaus didn't make this any easier than they had to. By the logic of the credit bureaus, they're in business to sell credit histories, not to give them out for free.

But the growing scourge of identity theft—and the fact that credit reports are sometimes the only way for consumers to discover they've been victims—prompted federal regulators to acknowledge that consumers should be encouraged to review their credit reports regularly.

Thanks to the Fair and Accurate Credit Transactions Act of 2003, consumers now have a much easier and cheaper time getting their credit reports. By September 2005, residents of all 50 states will have access to one free credit report per year from each of the "Big Three" agencies. But it's thanks to the Internet that getting a copy of your report has never been easier. The FACT Act forced the credit bureaus to set up a centralized Web site, where you can access your free annual report in just a few minutes.

Still, even with the new credit-report *glasnost,* other people have easier access to your reports than you do. You, for example, get free access to one credit report from each agency per year. After that, you'll pay up to $9.50 per report. Any credit professional can get the report faxed in minutes on the slightest pretense, with nothing more than your Social Security number or even your street address from the phone book, and often pay just pennies on the dollar to do it.

The same goes for your credit score, which lenders increasingly use as a quick determinant of whether to give you a thumbs-up or thumbs-down on credit. You'll pay at least a few dollars extra to get your score, while lenders pay far less.

There are three central credit bureaus that collect and resell the information in credit reports. These companies—Experian, TransUnion, and Equifax—repackage their files through their subsidiaries and hundreds of other data subcontractors. If you know what the three "superbureaus" are saying about you, then you know just about everything about your credit, save what the corner grocer says.

The reports that lenders and other creditors receive from the bureaus are formatted differently than those that consumers receive. If you're applying for a mortgage, you should read the advanced discussion of mortgage reports, which combine data from two or all three of the agencies, in **Advanced: Residential Mortgage Credit Reports** (page 92).

Also, don't be confused when the reporting agencies refer to credit reports as "consumer credit file disclosures." The agencies differentiate "disclosures" from the credit reports that lenders see, because there are certain entries that appear on the disclosure that lenders aren't allowed access to.

Specifically, any time a creditor or other entity checks your credit history in anticipation of offering you a loan, that credit inquiry will appear on the disclosure (that is, your consumer credit report). However, any inquiries that result from credit offers that you did not seek out—such as the slew of preapproved credit card offers mailed to consumers every year—will not show up on the lender's report.

But inquiries that result from your request for credit are visible to all, and too many such inquiries are often seen as a negative sign: Are you short on money and seeking it in many places recently? If you're preparing to apply for a major loan in coming months, resist the urge to apply for new credit cards now, no matter how good the deal sounds. The credit inquiries that end up on your report when you apply for credit could lower your credit score, and that will affect your monthly loan payment on that big loan for years to come.

NOTE ON CREDIT-MONITORING PRODUCTS

In recent years, lawmakers have forced the credit-reporting agencies to be more upfront with consumers and to make credit reports more accessible. That's a good thing, but it appears to have awakened the agencies' awareness of consumers as a rich source of additional profit. These days, visit the agencies' Web sites, and you'll be presented with an array of products. One popular pitch: Credit-monitoring tools.

These are useful for trumping identity theft fast. While they won't prevent your identity being stolen, these e-mail alert services let you know quickly when someone else has filched your data. The downside is they're expensive. To monitor your credit files at all three agencies could cost you up to $200 a year.

NOTE ON IDENTITY THEFT

Consumers who suspect they've been victims of identity theft can—and should—place a fraud alert on their credit report by making just one phone call to one credit reporting agency (for phone numbers, see Appendix III). That alert will make it more difficult for anyone to apply for credit in your name. No matter which agency you call, that agency is supposed to then notify the other two about your fraud alert. An initial fraud alert stays on your report for 90 days, and gives you access to one free report from each of the agencies.

An extended alert, which requires you to provide a copy of an identity-theft report filed with a law enforcement agency, stays for up to 7 years, and includes access to two free reports from each agency in the 12 months following the alert.

If you're filing an extended alert, consider filing it with all three agencies. While they're supposed to share the information among themselves, some industry experts note that these agencies are in competition with one another, and consumers may not want to rely on their ability to communicate among themselves.

NOTE ON CREDIT SCORES

When lenders or creditors pull your report, they also get a credit score, a number that is said to predict the likelihood of your defaulting on a loan in the future. Creditors, lenders, employers, insurance companies, and others use scores to determine whether or not to offer you credit, and what kind of interest rate and terms to give you.

The higher your score, the better deal you'll get, and the difference between a score of, say, 750 and a score of 650 could cost you thousands of dollars over your lifetime. It makes sense to buy your credit score before applying for a mortgage or other major loan. Unfortunately, lawmakers didn't take the opportunity during the FACT Act proceedings to ensure consumers would get access to free scores: You'll have to pay for your score.

The three bureaus each use unique analytical models to generate scores based on a consumer's credit history, and individual lenders and creditors often run their own models also, so the score used to judge you will vary depending on the lender. The most widely used score, though, is Fair Isaac Corp.'s FICO score, and the best way to get the score that most closely matches the number your lender is looking at is to get your FICO score. It's available at MyFico.com. Remember to get your FICO score for all three of your reports. Because the information on your reports will differ, so will the score generated on each report. With your three scores in hand, you'll have a better idea of what to expect when applying for credit.

While it's important to check your credit reports regularly to root out identity theft and credit errors (ideally, you should check your report from each agency at least once per year), your credit score is important only when you're about to make a change such as applying for a mortgage, car loan, or insurance policy or applying for a new job or renting a new apartment. Note that your score will change frequently, depending on when in the cycle you're checking it: Creditors follow different schedules when reporting your payment history to credit-reporting agencies. Don't fret too much about your score unless you're about to make the sort of change described above.

The strategies in this book are a way to clean up credit-report errors. Combine these strategies with the all-important habit of paying your bills on time, and your report should look great. But credit scores aren't always so simple. Sometimes what seems like a smart move regarding your finances can lead to a drop in your score.

For example, closing out old credit card accounts seems like a good way to tie up loose ends, right? But sometimes doing that can lower your credit score, because one factor used in score risk models is your payment history over time. If that credit card you closed had a good payment history that's now no longer being reported to the credit-reporting agencies, your score might drop.

Also, credit scoring takes into account the ratio of your total credit-card debt to your total available credit. That is, when you add up all your credit-card debt, you want that number to be relatively low when compared to the total dollars available to you if you maxed out all of your credit cards. Closing credit card accounts can make your debt-to-credit-limit ratio look worse.

Rather than trying to guess which actions might negatively affect your score, try the score simulator at MyFico.com. You can plug in theoretical situations to see how they affect your number. Remember that, like the credit-reporting agencies, Fair Isaac, Inc.—the company that developed the FICO score and operates the MyFico Web site—is in business to make money, so you'll be tempted by the myriad pricey products for sale at the site. The simulator and other calculators are free.

Steps to follow to get your credit report

1. Determine whether you have to pay for the reports. By September 2005, residents of all U.S. states and territories can go online to get one free report every 12 months from each of the three credit-reporting bureaus, as mandated by the Fair and Accurate Credit Transactions Act of 2003.

   Go to AnnualCreditReport.com to get your free report. Be careful when you type in the Web address: Some consumer advocates warn that scammers are creating similarly named but fraudulent sites to lure unsuspecting consumers to divulge personal information.

   Also, watch out for marketing ploys. For example, a site called FreeCreditReport.com is run by Experian. While it sounds a lot like the federally mandated one-stop shop for free reports, it's actually a 30-day free trial offer for the company's credit-monitoring product and does *not* provide you access to all three agencies' reports.

Don't bother going to the credit bureau Web sites to get your free annual reports, because they'll merely redirect you. You have to go to the centralized location. Once you get your report online, be sure to print it out *and* save it to your desktop with the "save file" feature. You want to print it out for perusing, and it's a good idea to save it, because data at the margins of the printed version may be cut off by the document formatting. Once you exit the Web site, you lose access to the report.

2. If you don't have Internet access, call 877-322-8228 to get your free reports. The bureaus must mail your report to you within 15 days. Or fill out an Annual Credit Report Request Form (see the next page) and mail it to Annual Credit Report Request Service, P.O. Box 105281, Atlanta, GA 30348-5281. If you don't want to use the form on the next page, you can pick up a Federal Trade Commission or AARP brochure with the form printed in it. Or you can go online to print out the form from the FTC Web site at http://www.ftc.gov/bcp/conline/edcams/credit/docs/fact_act_request_form.pdf

3. Gather your data. You'll need the following information at hand when you apply online, by phone or via mail: Your name, current address as well as any other addresses in the past two years, Social Security number, and date of birth.

Also, when you are ordering online, each of the bureaus will ask one or two security questions designed to ensure you are who you say you are. But because some of the data they have may be inaccurate, you might find it frustratingly difficult to answer the questions correctly.

For instance, the bureau might ask for your street address, but if it has the street spelled wrong in its files, you won't gain access to the site when you spell it correctly, and you'll have to choose an alter-

EQUIFAX   **experian**   **TransUnion.**

Annual Credit Report Request Form

You have the right to get a free copy of your credit file disclosure, commonly called a credit report, once every 12 months, from each of the nationwide consumer credit reporting companies - Equifax, Experian and TransUnion.

For instant access to your free credit report, visit www.annualcreditreport.com.

For more information on obtaining your free credit report, visit www.annualcreditreport.com or call 877-322-8228.

Use this form if you prefer to write to request your credit report from any, or all, of the nationwide consumer credit reporting companies. The following information is required to process your request. Omission of any information may delay your request.

Once complete, fold (do not staple or tape), place into a #10 envelope, affix required postage and mail to:
Annual Credit Report Request Service P.O. Box 105281 Atlanta, GA 30348-5281.

Please use a Black or Blue Pen and write your responses in PRINTED CAPITAL LETTERS without touching the sides of the boxes like the examples listed below.

A B C D E F G H I J K L M N O P Q R S T U V W X Y Z   0 1 2 3 4 5 6 7 8 9

Social Security Number: ☐☐☐ - ☐☐ - ☐☐☐☐

Date of Birth: ☐☐ / ☐☐ / ☐☐☐☐
Month   Day   Year

········ Fold Here ········   ········ Fold Here ········

First Name   M.I.

Last Name   JR, SR, III, etc.

Current Mailing Address:

House Number   Street Name

Apartment Number / Private Mailbox   For Puerto Rico Only: Print Urbanization Name

City   State   ZipCode

Previous Mailing Address (complete only if at current mailing address for less than two years):

House Number   Street Name

········ Fold Here ········   ········ Fold Here ········

Apartment Number / Private Mailbox   For Puerto Rico Only: Print Urbanization Name

City   State   ZipCode

Shade Circle Like This → ●   Not Like This → ⊗ ∅

I want a credit report from (shade each that you would like to receive):
○ Equifax
○ Experian
○ TransUnion

○ Shade here if, for security reasons, you want your credit report to include no more than the last four digits of your Social Security Number.

If additional information is needed to process your request, the consumer credit reporting company will contact you by mail.

Your request will be processed within 15 days of receipt and then mailed to you.

31238

nate security question. Or the bureau might request the name of all the creditors to which you owe student loans. Forget one name, and the bureau's system won't recognize you. You'll have to log out and try again.

4. If you've already received one free report from each agency within the past 12 months, there are special situations in which you are eligible for another free report.

   a. Some states offered residents one free report before the federal law went into effect. For most of those people, the federal law does not mean an additional report, just easier access to their free report through the central Web site. But Georgia promised its residents two free reports a year, and the federal law doesn't override that perk, so residents of Georgia can still get two free reports a year.

   b. If you've recently been rejected for a loan, or your insurance rates were raised due to information in your credit report, the lender or creditor is required to send you a "notice of adverse action," letting you know what happened and telling you which agency's report led to that action. You are then entitled to a free copy of that agency's file on you, as long as you request it within 60 days. See the **"Requesting Your Free Report If You Were Denied Credit"** letter (page 17).

   c. Other situations in which you're entitled to a free report are: You're unemployed and plan to apply for a job in the next 60 days; you're currently receiving public assistance; or you believe your file has inaccurate information due to fraud or because you've been a victim of identity theft.

5. If you've exhausted your access to free credit reports this year, you'll need to pay. Each agency allows you to buy your report online (see Web site addresses in Appendix I), and, per the FTC, can charge no more than $9.50 per report (as of this writing).

If you're about to apply for a loan, you'll also want to find out your credit score *from each agency,* because your score will vary depending on the information the bureau has collected on you.

Even though the credit-reporting agencies are pumping out slick-sounding credit scores—Experian has its Plus score, TransUnion its TrueCredit product—stick with the FICO score: It's the one most likely to match what lenders are looking at when they judge you.

While we dislike promoting any one particular credit-industry company, it's also true that one company's credit score dominates the industry. That's why consumers are often best off purchasing their three reports and FICO scores from Fair Isaac at My-Fico.com. That way you can be sure to get your FICO score based on each agency's report. Fair Isaac is currently charging about $45 for all three reports and scores, which is about what you'd pay ordering the reports individually ($9.50 for each of the three reports, plus at least $4 for each credit score, totals about $41).

Still, some state laws set a lower limit on how much the bureaus can charge for credit reports after consumers' access to free reports is exhausted, and residents of those states might consider purchasing their reports from each bureau individually, to save money.

As of this writing, in Minnesota, residents pay just $3, while in Connecticut, Maine, and Maryland the limit is $5. In Vermont, it's $7.50. California, Colorado, Massachusetts, and New Jersey set the limit at $8. In Montana, it's $8.50. For all other states, the top cost is $9.50. Georgia law ensures consumers receive two free reports a year, and after that, residents pay $9.50.

6. For those who don't have Internet access and have exhausted their access to free reports, the best bet is ordering your reports from each credit-reporting

agency directly, either by telephone or mail. See Appendix I for contact information. Copy out a version of Form Letter 1 three times, once for each of the companies. The companies keep separate files, so you should collect your files from all three. Be sure to:

- Use your full name, including any Jr. or Sr.
- Include your date of birth and Social Security number and telephone number
- For TransUnion, supply the name of your current employer
- Always use your present address, but include any other addresses for the previous two years
- Verify your identity; to do this, enclose copies of two bills—a utility bill, credit-card bill, and/or driver's license with your present address
- If you've changed your name (through marriage, for example), you should make note of this whenever identifying yourself to the credit bureaus
- Sign and date the letter

Protect yourself when you send these letters and all other letters in this book:

- Rephrase the letter in your own words; you don't want to appear like you are being coached or following a repair strategy
- Use *certified/return receipt* mail—it's an excellent way to prove that you sent a letter, and you don't need registered mail, which costs more
- Keep at least one photocopy of all correspondence you send to anyone
- Make a note of the day you sent off the report requests, so you can follow up if necessary

Form Letter 1: "Buying your credit report"

Credit bureau address
Date

To Customer Service:

Enclosed is my money order for *cost of credit report.*
Please send my credit report to the following address:

Your full name (include middle initial and any Jr. or Sr.)
Your address
Your Social Security number
Your birth date

You will also find enclosed documentation verifying
my identity. Thank you for your cooperation.

Sincerely,
Your signature

If the credit report doesn't come within 15 days of the bureau having received your request, mark an extra photocopy of the original credit-report request with your own version of the comment:

ATTENTION FTC:
It's been four weeks since I sent this letter certified/return receipt, and my credit report has not come yet!

Send this marked-up letter to the FTC (see Appendix IV for address), and send a photocopy to the credit bureau. Don't forget: Send all correspondence *certified/return receipt,* and keep photocopies for your own records.

"Requesting your free credit report if you were denied credit" letter

Use this letter if a credit report was used in a recent decision to deny you a loan or a job, raise your insurance rate or lower your credit limit. How do you know if a credit report was used? The institution that turned you down is required to tell you, via an "adverse action notice," whether your credit history was reviewed and also which credit bureau issued the report, although they are not required to provide you with a copy of the credit report. The credit bureau that issued the report is required to give you a free copy of your report if you request it within 60 days of being turned down.

Remember, when using this letter and all letters in this book, to:

1. Rephrase the letter in your own words. You don't want to appear like you are being coached or following a repair strategy.
2. Keep a photocopy of the letter for your records. The copies are often used later in the repair process.
3. Send the letter through *certified/return receipt* mail. Then you'll have proof that you sent the letter.

Credit bureau address
Date

To Customer Service:

I was recently rejected for a *loan, job, or insurance policy* by *name of rejecter* on *date of rejection*. The decision included use of a credit report from your service. I would like a copy of my report so I can look into this matter. Please send my credit report to the following address:

Your full name (include middle initial and any Jr. or Sr.)
Your address
Your Social Security number
Your birth date

(Continued)

> You will also find enclosed documentation verifying my identity. Thank you for your cooperation.
>
> Sincerely,
> *Your signature*

Advanced: Merged Reports and Residential Mortgage Credit Reports

The credit report used in evaluating your mortgage applications is special. You can't get ahold of it yourself, but you usually pay for it, and you should know what it contains. As part of the application process, the mortgage broker will ask you to explain any bad credit that appears in the report.

A merged or trimerged report is a combination of two or three credit-bureau reports, plus credit scores. The rules for mortgage applications warrant that two reports be combined as the basis for deciding your creditworthiness. Experian and TransUnion reports are a common combination, and some companies combine these two and Equifax. Depending on where you live, any combination is possible.

In effect, you can get your merged report by requesting reports from all three consumer-credit bureaus. Ask your mortgage broker, should you be in the process of applying, which bureaus are used for the merged report that the broker orders. This allows you to focus your credit disputes on the sources of your credit reports for your mortgage application.

A residential mortgage credit report goes one step further: An employee at a credit bureau reseller (these agencies work as middlemen between the Big Three reporting agencies and mortgage lenders) will check on the consumer by calling employers, landlords, current mortgage providers, and any creditors commented on or disputed in the mortgage application.

For an extra fee (though some lenders absorb this fee for prospective homebuyers), the credit agency reseller will perform a "rapid rescore," whereby inaccurate information on a report is disputed through a fast-track process at the credit bureau that published the information.

READ YOUR CREDIT REPORT

Introduction

Credit reports are much easier to read now than in the past, because years of pressure from consumer advocates and regulators led to significant changes in the credit-reporting industry.

The rise of identity theft was a key consideration for lawmakers when Congress wrote the Fair and Accurate Credit Transactions Act of 2003, which amends the Fair Credit Reporting Act. During that process, consumer advocates and others called attention to the growing importance of consumers understanding how the credit system works.

These days, bad marks on your credit report can determine whether you land the job you're applying for, how much you pay for auto and homeowners insurance, and your credit-card interest rate, plus whether you have to pay your utility or cell phone company a deposit.

But, despite tougher laws, including free reports for consumers, centralized fraud reporting, and more onus on creditors to respond to consumers' complaints, the credit-reporting industry is still, to a large degree, a black box, and credit reports are not nearly as clear and understandable as they could be. Consumers still get confused. If reading a credit report is unfamiliar to you, follow the step-by-step guide that follows.

This section focuses on identifying what's bad on your reports and the information you'll need for planning your repair effort. There are many different styles and formats of credit report, but most of them derive from one of the three super-bureaus that supplied the information being reported. Each of the three main credit bureaus uses a different format, plus each bureau's format varies depending on whether you request the report online or order it by phone or mail.

On top of that, regional credit bureaus, from which mortgage lenders and others often buy reports, use their own unique format to list your credit information. Nevertheless, the explanations in this section still apply. The instructions are organized around identifying the basic information you need for repairing bad credit:

- Credit name (and type of creditor)
- Account number
- Status
- Lateness patterns

Some of the information, such as your name and address, won't be new to you, but it's useful to know what the credit bureau has listed anyway. Tiny mistakes in any of the most mundane information can affect your credit rating, especially if it means you've been confused with someone else with a similar name.

Also, each credit bureau offers information on its Web site on how to read credit reports and how to submit a dispute, and also will mail you that information if you request your report by mail.

When communicating with the credit bureaus, be sure to include the credit report number at the top of your report. Experian calls it the "report number," TransUnion says "file number," and Equifax refers to it as a "confirmation number."

Identifying derogatory items

When you request your free annual report from Experian, you will get this version of your credit history (see sample on page 24). Its advantage is the plain language uses. Good credit items are listed in the section titled "accounts in good standing," and derogatory credit items will be listed under the "potentially negative" section. But don't let the word "potentially" fool you—these items are more than likely considered unfavorable by lenders and are lowering your credit score.

The disadvantage is that it may leave out valuable information for assessing your credit rating and challenging harmful elements of it. Specifically: While the account history for some credit accounts may be reported, there's no guarantee you'll get a complete history of payments. Without this, it's difficult to know when delinquencies were reported. You will have to get this information from the creditor.

On Experian reports, the account status terms that refer to "good," i.e. nonderogatory, credit items are "current account" and "paid satisfactorily." Even the innocuous-sounding "paid account" may include old derogatory items such as late payments. The older the late payments, the less they'll matter to your credit score and to lenders, but you still may want to assess their accuracy, and dispute them if they're wrong.

Your TransUnion report will look like the sample on page 30. Any negative credit items will be detailed under the heading "adverse accounts." TransUnion's online reports are visually easy to follow: Just look for any bracketed or shaded items on the account payment history. A box shaded yellow, orange, or red indicates a 30-day, 60-day, or 90-day late payment. On the black-and-white reports that TransUnion mails to consumers, those boxes are different shades of gray.

Equifax reports (see sample on page 35) offer detailed descriptions of its account status codes, and collection accounts and judgments or bankruptcies will be grouped near the top of the report, but negative credit items, such as a 90-day past due account, won't necessarily be grouped together.

Note that online report formats differ significantly from those that are mailed out, and from those that lenders see. On any credit report, some of the negative "account status" terms to look out for are listed below (these are the most common derogatory account status terms, but keep in mind that Experian alone says it uses more than 88 terms altogether).

Current, was 30: The account is now current but was past due 30 days at least once in the last 7 years.

Current, was 30-2: The account is now current but was 30 days late twice.

Past due 30, 60, 90, or 120 days: This account is past due the specified number of days.

Closed account: Make sure that if the account was closed by you that your report says "closed by consumer." Some lenders consider an account closed by the creditor as a negative.

Delinquency: This can mean a late account was sent to collection.

Judgment/civil claim: A creditor sued you to try to collect payment.

Bankruptcy: You filed bankruptcy. This negative mark can stay on your report for up to 10 years.

Collection or collection account: A past-due account that the creditor passed off to a collection agency.

Charge-offs: A charge-off is an account that was written off as a loss for tax purposes by the creditor. A charge-off can be for a very small amount of money, but no matter how small, it is severely damaging to your credit. Many charge-offs come from additional account charges, accounts with only a few dollars owing, or annual fees that accrue whether you know it or not. When you fail to pay, they charge it off, usually automatically, when tax time comes. They win small, you lose big. A "paid charge off" is one that you've paid. Even though the debt is settled, this credit status is almost as bad as a charge-off.

Other codes to watch for include the following: "R" means a revolving credit line, such as a credit card, while "I" stands for an installment loan, such as an auto or student loan. "M" might be used for mortgage, and "O" is a pay-every-month account, such as American Express.

The smaller the number, the better the news, so an "R1" means a revolving account in good standing, while an "R7" is an account with a 180-days late payment.

Identifying the status date

There may be a few different dates on a consumer credit report, most of which are not important to the credit-repair process. The status date is important: It indicates the last time your file was updated to include account status terms such as "was 30 days late."

The status date helps you determine how to dispute an item. A status date older than a year indicates that an account is likely no longer active. Records for accounts with these older status dates may be kept in archives, and this is a boon to anyone who is disputing bad credit. Creditors are often loath to look up archival information, and some make it a policy to ignore disputes on old paid accounts.

Even if the status date is for the most recent month, this does not mean that your bad credit results from that month. The account history section gives you the best idea of when your bad credit marks were added to the file.

Experian Credit Report Sample

Online Personal Credit Report from Experian

Experian credit report prepared for
JOHN Q CONSUMER
Your report number is
1562064065
Report Date:
01/24/2005

Experian collects and organizes information about you and your credit history from public records, your creditors and other reliable sources. Experian makes your credit history available to your current and prospective creditors, employers and others as allowed by law, which can expedite your ability to obtain credit and can make offers of credit available to you. We do not grant or deny credit; each credit grantor makes that decision based on its own guidelines.

Potentially Negative Items

Public Records

Credit grantors may carefully review the items listed below when they check your credit history. Please note that the account information connected with some public records, such as bankruptcy, also may appear with your credit items listed later in this report.

MAIN COUNTY CLERK

Address:	Identification Number:	Plaintiff:
123 MAINTOWN S BUFFALO, NY 10000	1	ANY COMMISSIONER O.

Status:	Status Details:
Civil Claim paid.	This item was verified and updated on 06/2001.

Date Filed:	Claim Amount:
10/15/2000	$200
Date Resolved:	Liability Amount:
01/04/2001	NA

Responsibility:
INDIVIDUAL

Credit Items

For your protection, the last few digits of your account numbers do not display.

ABCD BANKS

Address:
100 CENTER RD
BUFFALO, NY 10000
(555) 555-5555

Account Number:
1000000. . . .

Status: **Paid/Past due 60 days**

Date Opened: 10/1997	Type: Installment	Credit Limit/Original Amount: $523
Reported Since: 11/1997	Terms: 12 Months	High Balance: NA
Date of Status: 01/1999	Monthly Payment: $0	Recent Balance: $0 as of 01/1999
Last Reported: 01/1999	Responsibility: Individual	Recent Payment: $0

Account History:
60 days as of 12/1998
30 days as of 11/1998

MAIN COLL AGENCIES

Address:
PO BOX 123
ANYTOWN, PA 10000
(555) 555-5555

Account
Number:
0123456789

Original Creditor:
TELEVISE CABLE COMM.

Status: **Collection account. $95 past due as of 04/2000.**

Date Opened: 01/2000	Type: Installment	Credit Limit/Original Amount: $95
Reported Since: 04/2000	Terms: NA	High Balance: NA
Date of Status: 04/2000	Monthly Payment: $0	Recent Balance: $95 as of 04/2000
Last Reported: 04/2000	Responsibility: Individual	Recent Payment: $0

Your statement: **ITEM DISPUTED BY CONSUMER**
Account History:
Collection as of 4/2000

Accounts in Good Standing

AUTOMOBILE AUTO FINANCE

Address:	Account Number:	
100 MAIN ST E	12345678998. . . .	
SMALLTOWN, MD 90001		
(555) 555-5555		

Status: **Open/Never late.**

Date Opened:	Type:	Credit Limit/Original Amount:
01/2000	**Installment**	$10,355
Reported Since:	Terms:	High Balance:
01/2000	**65 Months**	NA
Date of Status:	Monthly	Recent Balance:
08/2001	Payment:	$7,984 as of 08/2001
	$210	
Last Reported:	Responsibility:	Recent Payment:
08/2001	**Individual**	$0

MAIN

Address:	Account Number:	
PO BOX 1234	1234567899876	
FORT LAUDERDALE, FL 10009		

Status: **Closed/Never late.**

Date Opened:	Type:	Credit Limit/Original Amount:
03/1991	Revolving	NA
Reported Since:	Terms:	High Balance:
03/1991	1 Month	$3,228
Date of Status:	Monthly	Recent Balance:
08/2000	Payment:	$0/paid as of 08/2000
	$0	
Last Reported:	Responsibility:	Recent Payment:
08/2000	Individual	$0

Your statement: **Account closed at consumer's request**

Requests for Your Credit History

Requests Viewed by Others

We make your credit history available to your current and prospective creditors and employers as allowed by law. Personal data about you may be made available to companies whose products and services may interest you.

The section below lists all who have requested in the recent past to review your credit history as a result of actions involving you, such as the completion of a credit application or the transfer of an account to a collection agency, mortgage or loan application, etc. Creditors may view these requests when evaluating your creditworthiness.

HOMESALE REALTY CO

Address: Date of Request:
2000 S MAINROAD BLVD STE   07/16/2001
ANYTOWN CA 11111
(555) 555-5555
Comments: Real estate loan on behalf of 1000 CORPORATE COMPANY. This inquiry is scheduled to continue on record until 8/2003.

ABC BANK

Address: Date of Request:
PO BOX 100   02/23/2001
BUFFALO NY 10000
(555) 555-5555
Comments: Permissible purpose. This inquiry is scheduled to continue on record until 3/2003.

ANYTOWN FUNDING INC

Address: Date of Request:
100 W MAIN AVE STE 100   07/25/2000
INTOWN CA 10000
(555) 555-5555
Comments: Permissible purpose. This inquiry is scheduled to continue on record until 8/2002.

Requests Viewed Only by You

The section below lists all who have a permissible purpose by law and have requested in the recent past to review your information. You may not have initiated these requests, so you may not recognize each source. We offer information about you to those with a permissible purpose, for example, to:

- other creditors who want to offer you preapproved credit;
- an employer who wishes to extend an offer of employment;
- a potential investor in assessing the risk of a current obligation;
- Experian or other credit reporting agencies to process a report for you;
- your existing creditors to monitor your credit activity (date listed may reflect only the most recent request).

We report these requests **only to you** as a record of activities. We **do not** provide this information to other creditors who evaluate your creditworthiness.

MAIN BANK USA
Address: Date of Request:
1 MAIN CTR AA 11   08/10/2001
BUFFALO NY 10000

MAINTOWN BANK
Address: Date of Request:
PO BOX 100   08/05/2001
MAINTOWNS DE 10000
(555) 555-5555

ANYTOWN DATA CORPS
Address: Date of Request:
2000 S MAINTOWN BLVD STE   07/16/2001
INTOWN CO 11111
(555) 555-5555

Personal Information

The following information is reported to us by you, your creditors and other sources. Each source may report your personal information differently, which may result in variations of your name, address, Social Security number, etc. As part of our fraud-prevention program, a notice with additional information may appear. As a security precaution, the Social Security number that you used to obtain this report is not displayed. The Geographical Code shown with each address identifies the state, county, census tract, block group and Metropolitan Statistical Area associated with each address.

Names: Address:
JOHN Q CONSUMER   123 MAIN STREET
JONATHON Q CONSUMER   ANYTOWN, MD 90001-9999
J Q CONSUMER   Type of Residence: Multifamily
                                        Geographical Code: 0-156510-31-8840

Social Security number variations: Address: 555 SIMPLE PLACE
999999999   ANYTOWN, MD 90002-7777
                                        Type of Residence: Single family
                                        Geographical Code: 0-176510-33-8840

Year of birth:
1954

Employers:
ABCDE ENGINEERING CORP

Telephone numbers:
(555) 555 5555 Residential

Address: 999 HIGH DRIVE APT 15B
ANYTOWN, MD 90003-5555
Type of Residence: Single family
Geographical Code: 0-156510-31-8840

Your Personal Statement

No general personal statements appear on your report.

Important Message from Experian

By law, we cannot disclose certain medical information (relating to physical, mental, or behavioral health or condition). Although we do not generally collect such information, it could appear in the name of a data furnisher (i.e., "Cancer Center") that reports your payment history to us. If so, those names display in your report, but in reports to others they display only as MEDICAL PAYMENT DATA. Consumer statements included on your report at your request that contain medical information are disclosed to others.

Contacting Us

Contact address and phone number for your area will display here.

TransUnion Credit Report Sample

Personal Information

Name: EXAMPLE TEST USER

File Number: 123456789

You have been on our files since 05/1999

Date Issued: Nov 16, 2004

SSN: XXX-XX-0001

Telephone: (555) 555-1234x12345

Your SSN is partially masked for your protection

CURRENT ADDRESS

Address: 1100 CURRENT ST
                  PERCITY, CA 10000

Reported: 09/2002

EMPLOYMENT DATA REPORTED

Employer Name: EMPLOYER 1

Position: JOB/OCCUPATION 1

Date Reported: 06/2004

Hired: 05/2004

Special Notes: Your Social Security number has been masked for your protection. You may request disclosure of the full number by writing to us at the address found at the end of this report. Also, any item on your credit report that begins with 'MED1' indicates medical information. The data following this word is not displayed to anyone but you, except where permitted by law.

Public Records

The following items obtained from public records appear on your report. You may be required to explain public record items to potential creditors. Any bankruptcy information will remain on your report for 10 years from the date of the filing. Unpaid tax liens may generally be reported for an indefinite period of time depending on your state of residence. Paid tax liens may be reported for 7 years from the date of payment. All other public record information, including discharged chapter 13 bankruptcy and any accounts containing adverse information, remain for up to 7 years.

CRCITY MUNICIPAL   Docket#: 95C00558

222 E. MAIN   Type: Civil Judgment   Date Filed: 12/2002

SUITE 101   Court Type: Municipal   Responsibility: Participant

CRCITY, CA 40003   on account

(555) 111-2222

Date Paid: 07/2004　　　Plaintiff: **BANK OF NEW YORK**
Assets: $1,079　　　　　Plaintiff Attorney: **PERRY MASON**
　　　　　　　　　　　　Amount: **$1,079**
Estimated date that this item will be removed: **06/2009**

Key to reading your payment history data.

Some creditors report how you make payments each month in relation to your agreement with them. The key below outlines how to read the payment history section for each account:

N/A	OK	30	60	90	120
N/A Unknown	Current	30 days late	60 days late	90 days late	120 days late

Adverse Accounts

The following accounts contain certain information which some creditors may consider to be adverse. Adverse account information may generally be reported for 7 years from the date of the first delinquency, depending on your state of residence. The adverse information in these accounts has been printed in >brackets< or is shaded for your convenience, to help you understand your report. They are not bracketed or shaded this way for creditors. (Note: The account # may be scrambled by the creditor for your protection.)

R DEPARTMENT ONE　#0000000000000001

4401 E. CREDITOR S ST SUITE401
CR CITY, CA 40001
(800) 555-4000

Balance:	$153	Pay Status:	Paid or Paying as Agreed
Updated:	07/2004	Account Type:	Revolving account
High Balance:	$532	Responsibility:	Individual account
Opened:	01/1999	Credit Limit:	$5,000
Past Due:	$0	Loan Type:	Appliance/Furniture

	30	60	90
Late Payments (last 48 months)	2	0	0

Last 4 Years

OK	OK	OK	OK	OK	OK	OK	OK	OK	OK	OK	OK	OK	OK	OK	OK
aug	jul	jun	may	apr	mar	feb	'02	dec	nov	oct	sep	aug	jul	jun	may

OK	OK	OK	OK	OK	OK	OK	OK	OK	30	OK	OK	OK	OK	OK	OK
apr	mar	feb	'01	dec	nov	oct	sep	aug	jul	jun	may	apr	mar	feb	'00

OK	OK	OK	OK	OK	OK	OK	OK	OK	OK	30	OK	OK	OK	OK	OK
dec	nov	oct	sep	aug	jul	jun	may	apr	mar	feb	'99	dec	nov	oct	sep

Satisfactory Accounts

The following accounts are reported with no adverse information.

OTHER FINANCE ONE #000000002
4402 E. CREDITOR S ST SUITE402
CRCITY, CA 40001
(800) 555-4001

Balance:	$0	Pay Status:	Paid or Paying as Agreed
Updated:	07/2004	Account Type:	Installment account
High Balance:	$20,000	Responsibility:	Individual account
Opened:	05/1999	Credit Limit:	$0
Past Due:	$0		

	30	60	90
Late Payments (last 61 months)	0	0	0

Last 4 Years

OK	OK	OK	OK	OK	OK	OK	OK	OK	OK	OK	OK	OK	OK	OK	OK
jun	may	apr	mar	feb	'04	dec	nov	oct	sep	aug	jul	jun	may	apr	mar
OK	OK	OK	OK	OK	OK	OK	OK	OK	OK	OK	OK	OK	OK	OK	OK
feb	'03	dec	nov	oct	sep	aug	jul	jun	may	apr	mar	feb	'02	dec	nov
OK	OK	OK	OK	OK	OK	OK	OK	OK	OK	OK	OK	OK	OK	OK	OK
oct	sep	aug	jul	jun	may	apr	mar	feb	'01	dec	nov	oct	sep	aug	jul

CREDIT CARD CO #000000003
1111 N FAKESTREET WY
CRCITY, CA 40001
(800) 555-4002

Balance:	$0	Pay Status:	Paid or Paying as Agreed
Updated:	07/2004	Account Type:	Revolving account
High Balance:	$4,000	Responsibility:	Individual account
Opened:	03/2000	Credit Limit:	$6,000
Past Due:	$0		

	30	60	90
Late Payments (last 51 months)	0	0	0

Last 4 Years

OK	OK	OK	OK	OK	OK	OK	OK	OK	OK	OK	OK	OK	OK	OK	OK
jun	may	apr	mar	feb	'04	dec	nov	oct	sep	aug	jul	jun	may	apr	mar
OK	OK	OK	OK	OK	OK	OK	OK	OK	OK	OK	OK	OK	OK	OK	OK
feb	'03	dec	nov	oct	sep	aug	jul	jun	may	apr	mar	feb	'02	dec	nov
OK	OK	OK	OK	OK	OK	OK	OK	OK	OK	OK	OK	OK	OK	OK	OK
oct	sep	aug	jul	jun	may	apr	mar	feb	'01	dec	nov	oct	sep	aug	jul

Regular Inquiries

The following companies have received your credit report. Their inquiries remain on your credit report for two years.

INQUIRY ANALYSIS NAME 1
5501 NW INQUIRY E ST #501
INCITY, CA 50001

Requested on: 10/2004   Permissible Purpose: Employment
Inquiry Type: Individual Account

EXAMPLE INQUIRY COMPANY
1234 S CREDIT ST #123
ANYTOWN, IL 12345

Requested on: 6/2004   Permissible Purpose: Credit Transaction
Inquiry Type: Individual Account

Inquiry Analysis

The companies that request your credit report must first provide certain information about you. Within the past 90 days, companies that requested your report provided the following information.

INQUIRY ANALYSIS NAME 1

Requested on: 10/2004
Identifying Information They Provided: EXAMPLE TEST USER
                                         1100 CURRENT ST
                                         PERCITY, CA 10001

Promotional Inquiries

The companies listed below received your name, address and other limited information about you so they could make a firm offer of credit or insurance. They did not receive your full credit report, and these inquiries are not seen by anyone but you.

SAMPLE BANK
5678 MAIN RD
SUITE 123
SOME CITY, VA 98765
(800) 555-5555

Requested on: 03/05/2003

Account Review Inquiries

The companies listed below obtained information from your consumer report for the purpose of an account review or other business transaction with you. These inquiries are not displayed to anyone but you and will not affect any creditor's decision or any score (except insurance companies may have access to other insurance company inquiries, where permitted by law).

OTHER FINANCE ONE
4402 E CREDITOR ST
CRCITY, CA 40001
(800) 555-4001

Requested on:	11/01/2002
Inquiry Type:	Individual

SAMPLE INSURANCE CO
1111 N FAKESTREET WY
CRCITY, CA 40002
(800) 555-4002

Requested on:	05/01/2004	Permissible Purpose:	Insurance Underwriting
Inquiry Type:	Individual		

Consumer Statement
My wallet was stolen on June 19, 2004. Please ask for identification when you receive an application for credit.
(Note: This statement is set to expire in 12/2004.)

Special Messages
Security Alert: #HK#CACRA Consumer's identity may have been used without his or her consent. Recipients of this report are advised to verify the consumer's identity prior to issuing credit. Verify at 805 555-1212.
(Note: This statement is set to expire in 12/2004.)

Note: This report example is only an illustration of the type of information provided when your TransUnion Personal Credit Report is ordered. The information in the report does not reflect your personal situation. You must order your TransUnion Personal Credit Report to obtain the credit information that pertains to your personal situation.

Equifax Credit™ Report Sample

Personal Information

This credit report is available for you to view until <date>. This report will not update. If you would like a credit report as of a later date, you may order another one in the Member Center.

The following information is added to your file either when creditors enter requests to view your credit history, or when you report it to Equifax directly. If you believe that any of this information is incorrect, please see the Dispute File Information section at the end of this report.

Name: Stephen X. Smith Jr.
Social Security Number: 123-45-6789
Age or Date of Birth: May 1, 1965
Formerly Known As:
Death Notice:

Current Address
123 Penny Lane
Anytown, PA 12345
Date Reported 01/2001

Previous Address
Former Address 1
345 Easy Street
Anytown, VA 23456
Date Reported 01/2001

Former Address 2
678 Boardwalk
Anytown, NC 23456
Date Reported 01/2001

Other Identification

Date Reported	Type Code	Identification Number	Reason
MM/YYYY	Tax ID	12-3456789	Employee ID Number
MM/YYYY	SIN	446-68-7338	
MM/YYYY	Social Security Number	344-58-7666	Variation
MM/YYYY	Social Security Number	244-98-2297	Freeze

Employment History
Last Reported Employment:
Director; ACME; Atlanta, GA; Since: 01/2001; Until: 11/2004; Verified: 11/2004

Previous Employment(s):
Manager; ACME; Atlanta, GA; Since: 02/1999; Until: 01/2001; Verified: 01/2001
Associate; ACME; Atlanta, GA; Since: 03/1998; Until: 02/1999; Verified: 01/1999

Alert(s)
File Blocked For Promotional Purposes
ID Theft Victim—Information Blocked Due To Police or DMV Report
Security Freeze In Place

Fraud Alert
Expiration Date:	Date Reported:
Address:	Phone:
Phone:	Phone:
Comments:	

Active Duty Alert
Expiration Date:	Date Reported:
Address:	Phone:
Phone:	Phone:
Comments:	

Consumer Statement
The following Consumer Statement was added on 09/1999 and will expire on 09/2006:
This is the statement a consumer may add to their file.

Credit Summary
The following information is a summary of the Account Information in this report. To view your accounts in full detail, see the Account Information section. If you believe that any of this information is incorrect, please see the Dispute File Information section at the end of this report. This information is a snapshot in time and reflects account statuses and balances as of the date shown above.

Type of Account	Number of Accounts	Total Balance of Accounts
Mortgage	1	$150,000
Installment	6	$5,000
Revolving	14	$8,000
Other	1	$2,800
Total Accounts	22	$165,800

Number of Open Accounts	6
Number of Closed Accounts	15
Total Accounts in Good Standing	22
Accounts Currently Past Due	0
Negative Account History	0
Inquiries in Last 12 Months	2

Account Information Summary

Account Name	Account Type	Account Number	Date Opened
ABC Lending Co	Revolving	98765432109XXXX	04/1998
CAR $10,000 Loan Group	Installment	292832847XXXX	09/1999
123 Mortgage Company	Installment	92872625253XXXX	07/2000
XYZ Bankcard	Revolving	1234455-938XXXX	11/1990
ABC Lending Co	Revolving	98765432109XXXX	04/1998

Balance	Date Reported	Past Due	Account Status	Credit Limit
$3,500	09/2002	n/a	Pays or Paid as Agreed	$10,000
$4,857	08/2002	n/a	Pays or Paid as Agreed	$10,000
$149,000	09/2002	n/a	Pays or Paid as Agreed	$10,000
$2,876	08/2002	$102	30 days past due	$10,000
$3,500	09/2002	n/a	Pays or Paid as Agreed	$10,000

Other Accounts

Account Name	Account Number	Date Opened	Balance
American Express	372582760XXXX	10/1999	$2,800

Date Reported	Past Due	Account Status	Credit Limit
09/2002	n/a	Pays or Paid as Agreed	$10,000

Accounts Currently Past Due

Account Name	Account Number	Date Opened	Balance
XYZ Bankcard	1234455938XXXX	11/1990	$2,876

Date Reported	Past Due	Account Status	Credit Limit
08/2002	$102	30 days past due	$10,000

Inquiries

Inquiries that display to companies and may impact your credit score. This section lists companies that requested your credit file. Credit grantors may view these requests when evaluating your credit worthiness. Employment inquiries do not impact your credit score.

Name of Company	Date of Inquiry
Duke Electric	11/17/01
Ford Credit	04/17/02

Inquiries that do not display to companies and do not impact your credit score. This section includes inquiries which display only to you and are not considered when evaluating your credit worthiness. Examples of this inquiry type include a pre-approved offer of credit, insurance, or periodic account review by an existing creditor.

Name of Company	Date of Inquiry	Type of Inquiry
Citifinancial	09/09/02	AM
MBNA	08/18/02, 05/18/02, 02/18/02, 11/18/01, 08/18/01, 05/18/01	AR
BellSouth Wireless	08/03/02	PRM
123 Mortgage Company	08/18/02, 02/18/02, 08/18/01	AR
Promotional Inquiry	08/03/02	PRM
Prescreen Inquiry	08/18/02	PRM
Equifax Consumer Services	01/01/01	ID

Types of Inquiries

PRM	A promotional inquiry in which your name and address were given to a lender for credit offers, such as credit card solicitations. These inquiries remain on your file for 12 months.
AM or AR	An Account Monitoring or Account Review inquiry in which one of your creditors performs a periodic review of your account. These inquiries remain on your file for 12 months.
Equifax, ID, ACIS or UPDATE	Internal inquiries, which indicate Equifax's activity in response to your contact with us, for either a copy of your credit report or a request for research. These inquiries will remain on your file for 24 months.

Collections

A collection is an account that has been turned over to a collection agency by one of your creditors because you have not paid the account as agreed. If you believe that any of this information is incorrect, please see the Dispute File Information section at the end of this report.

ABC Lending Co

Agency Address:	123 Easy Street
	Anytown, GA 33333
	Phone Number: 555-555-5555
Date Reported:	05/1996
Date Assigned:	06/1996
Creditor Classification:	Retail
Creditor Name:	Sears
Account Number:	1234123412341234
Account Owner:	Stephen X. Smith
Original Amount Owed:	$1400.00
Date of 1st Delinquency:	05/1995
Balance Date:	06/1996
Balance Owed:	$1150.00
Last Payment Date:	04/1996
Status Date:	07/1996
Status:	Unsettled
Comments:	Reinvestigation in Progress

Public Records

Public record information includes bankruptcies, liens or judgments and comes from federal, state or county court records. If you believe that any of this information is incorrect, please see the Dispute File Information section at the end of this report.

Bankruptcy or Wage Earner Plan

Date Filed:	01/2003
Case Number:	1A223344567
Court Number/Name:	12-Anywhere Court House
Court Address:	123 Easy Street
	Anytown, GA 33333
	Phone Number: 555-555-5555
Liabilities:	$25,000
Individual/Joint:	Joint
Individual/Business:	Business
Bankruptcy Disposition:	CH-12, Discharged
Current Disposition Date:	11/17/2004
Asset Amount:	$36,000

Exempt Amount: $23,000
Date Verified: 11/18/2004
Date Reported: 11/25/2004
Prior Disposition: Discharged CH12
Comments: Reinvestigation in Progress

Suits or Judgments

Type: Judgment
Date Filed: 10/13/2003
Case Number: 998877665544
Court Number/Name: 11-Anytime Court House
Court Address: 123 Easy Street
                        Anytown, GA 33333
                        Phone Number: 555-555-5555
Plaintiff: Mr. Plaintiff
Defendant: Mr. Defendant
Amount: $2,500.00
Status: Verified
Date Reported: 10/15/2003
Satisfied Date: 11/17/2003
Verified Date: 11/25/2004
Comments: Consumer Disputes

Tax Lien

Date Filed: 05/2001
Case Number: 334456567878
Court Number/Name: 33-Anycity Court House
Court Address: 123 Easy Street
                        Anytown, GA 33333
                        Phone Number: 555-555-5555
Amount: $1,500.00
Class: Anycounty, Anytown
Date Reported: 06/25/2001
Lien Status: Unreleased
Date Released: 08/25/2002
Date Verified: 09/29/2002
Comments: Consumer says never late

REPAIR YOUR CREDIT REPORT

Introduction: Basic and Advanced

By this point in the steps to repairing your credit rating, you have received and decoded your credit reports from the three major credit bureaus. You have identified the harmful information they are reporting on you, and you are ready to change it.

The repair process is divided into two sections. The first, **basic,** takes you through the process of written disputes with credit bureaus. The second, **advanced,** gives you a strategic perspective on the fastest and most effective dispute techniques for different combinations of bad credit. The techniques counseled in the **advanced** section include when to rely on the **basic** instructions, but also include creditor negotiation, rapid rescoring, and use of the Fair Credit Reporting Act and Fair Credit Billing Act.

The **basic** disputes are straightforward and will work very well for the majority of derogatory credit items, but they are slow. At the minimum, disputes with the credit bureaus will take one to two months.

If you're not succeeding with the credit bureaus alone, or you want to plan the smartest, fastest, most effective course of action at the outset, make sure to also read the **advanced** section. The main focus of the **advanced** section is negotiating with creditors as opposed to the **basic** technique of challenging the credit bureaus.

Basic credit bureau disputes

Most credit repair is done by disputing derogatory items with the three main credit bureaus. But it makes sense to dispute erroneous credit report items with the relevant creditors as well as the credit reporting agencies.

The simple secret to the techniques described in the section on basic credit-bureau disputes is: *The credit bureaus often don't have the time or inclination to substantiate the validity of information they report when you challenge them.*

The laziness of the credit bureaus creates a bad system— imagine all the mistakes they make, not bothering to check the information they resell!—but it's one that you can turn to your advantage. If you demand that the credit bureaus perform at the level implied by the appropriate regulation, they will often clear the record rather than spend time and resources picking over an individual issue. The system cannot ordinarily handle people who won't take no for an answer.

A downside, for consumers, is that the system is in large part automated. When you dispute an item, the credit bureau checks that item with the creditor. Some creditors simply check their database to verify that the item matches what they furnished the agency. If it matches, the creditor verifies the item. That means any incorrect items in the creditor's database may continue to be reported on your credit report. In those cases, you'll have to dispute the item with the creditor.

Step-by-Step Basic Credit-Bureau Disputes

The steps that follow for disputing derogatory items with the three major credit bureaus are straightforward. They essentially involve sending a series of letters to each of the credit bureaus.

If you're in a hurry, it's faster to dispute derogatory items online or via telephone. However, if you can take the extra time, it's best to correspond via mail. That way you can keep copies of all pertinent letters, plus have evidence that the credit reporting agency received your letters (make sure you send all letters *certified/return receipt*). See Appendix II for information on contacting the three major credit-reporting agencies to dispute credit-report information.

Also, if you're applying for a mortgage loan, your mortgage broker or lender may be willing to do what's called a "rapid rescoring." With rapid rescoring, you present any evidence you have that the negative information on your report is inaccurate to the lender's credit reseller, the company through which they buy credit reports for judging loan applicants.

For a fee, the credit reseller can within a few days get the erroneous negative information corrected at the credit-reporting agency. Then the mortgage lender pulls your report again, which now, with the negative information removed, will show a new, improved credit score. Some lenders, but not all, pass the fee for this service on to the consumer, so, expect to pay as much as $45 per erroneous credit item.

When disputing via the standard method, if you have three or fewer credit items to dispute, use the **Basic System for Disputing Three or Fewer Items** (page 45); if you have more, use the **Basic System for Disputing Four or More Items** (page 48).

Often the credit bureaus will throw obstacles in your way. Here is exactly how not to take no for an answer, and to move step by step through a process that was designed by the credit bureaus to wear out your patience and make you quit.

If, at the end of the series of letters, you are not successful (unlikely in simple cases, likely in severe situations), go to the **advanced** section on creditor disputes.

There are five escalating letters in this **basic** section:

1. The initial dispute
2. The second notice (to hurry response to the initial dispute)
3. Demand letter 1 (if no items are corrected)
4. Demand letter 2 (if some items but not all are corrected)
5. The secondary dispute letter (after some success, to dispute more items)

The basic-dispute process is organized around the letters. The instructions for executing each letter are included with a sample of each letter on the following pages. The letters are only useful if you trace your progress on the following **Basic Dispute Flowchart,** because the timing of the letters is as important as what they say.

Basic Dispute Flowchart

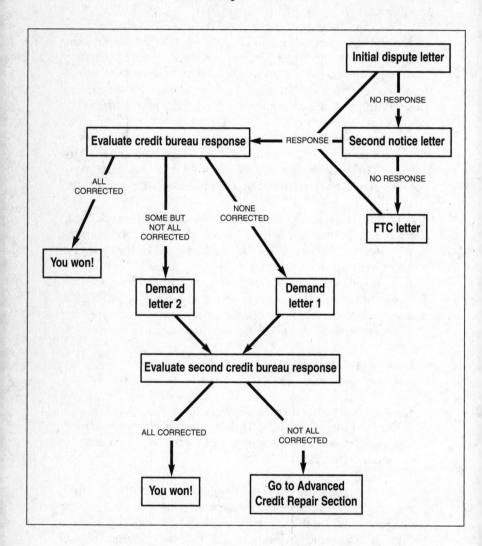

Basic System for Disputing Three or Fewer Items

You have to get your credit report from each of the credit bureaus, because they're separate reporting agencies, because they often report different things, and because you can't know which report someone is going to use to deny you credit. This means you have to dispute similar items on different credit reports, credit bureau by credit bureau.

Clearing an item on one bureau's report won't clear it off another. (In cases of identity theft, a dispute process initiated at one bureau is supposed to clean up the mess at all three agencies, but it's best not to rely on that. You should dispute errors arising from identity theft with all three agencies.)

The good news is that if you succeed in clearing an item off one report, it's an indication that you'll likely succeed with another credit bureau. When you have three or fewer items to dispute with each of the bureaus, conduct the disputes concurrently.

1. Send **initial dispute letter** (page 52).

2. Thirty days after Step 1, send **second-notice letter** (page 55). (The credit bureaus are required by the Fair Credit Reporting Act to respond within 30 days, though they get an additional 15 days if you submit additional documentation supporting your claim within that 30-day period.)

3. If, 10 days after Step 2, the credit bureaus still haven't responded, send the **FTC dispute letter** (page 64) with a copy of your **second-notice letter** to both the FTC and the credit bureaus.

4. When you get a response from the credit bureaus, there are three possibilities:
   a. If they remove *all* the derogatory items that you disputed, *you won!* The credit repair is complete.
      How to recognize this response. The credit bureaus will send you a letter describing the action they took, plus either a new version of your credit

report or an abbreviated version showing the status of any trade lines associated with the dispute. Make sure that the credit bureaus now refer to the disputed items as one of the following:

paid account
paid as agreed
current account
paid satisfactorily
open/never late
closed/never late (as long as the account was "closed by consumer"; accounts closed by the creditor are a negative mark)

On TransUnion's reports, the items that were bracketed or shaded yellow, orange, or red, or different shades of gray, to show a 30-day, 60-day, or 90-day late payment should now either have no brackets or be green and say "OK."

Note: Make sure that the changed item is now harmless. Sometimes, the credit bureaus will simply change it to a lesser derogatory. (See **Read Your Credit Report** for information on decoding your report.)

What to do next? Nothing. You've won!

b. The second possibility is they remove some but not all of the derogatory items that you disputed. *Don't settle for halfway.* Go to Step 5.

How to recognize this response. The credit bureaus will send you a letter describing the action they took, plus either a new version of your credit report, or an abbreviated version showing the status of any trade lines associated with the dispute. Any item that has not been corrected will either simply remain on the report, will say "item remains, confirmed by source," "verified as reported," or the negative item may be changed to a lesser degree of lateness.

What to do next? Send **demand letter 2** (page 59) to redispute the uncorrected items with stronger language and an explanation that is rooted in your consumer rights. This works, because your more specific complaints force the credit bureau to choose between an expensive investigation and clearing your credit. The credit bureaus have a limited number of roadblocks they're willing to enforce, and if you've gotten to this point, you've already broken through one.

c. The third possibility is none of the items are corrected. Don't be frustrated. This is a common result of the automatic verification that occurs when the agency asks the creditor about the item. If the item is wrong in the creditor's database, it often comes back as "verified." Go to the **advanced** section to find out how to negotiate with your creditor.

   How to recognize this response. The credit bureaus will send you an abbreviated credit update or credit report that says "items remain confirmed" or "verified as reported," or the disputed items will simply remain unchanged.

   What to do next? Send **demand letter 1** (page 57) to redispute the uncorrected items with stronger language that is rooted in your consumer rights. This works because your more specific complaints force the credit bureau to choose between an expensive investigation and clearing your credit. The credit bureaus have a limited number of roadblocks they're willing to enforce, and if you've gotten to this point, you've already broken through one.

5. This step is only needed if you sent a **demand letter** (see 4b or 4c, above). Just as above—when you got a response from the credit bureau to your **initial dispute letter**—there are three possible responses from the credit bureau to your **demand letter:**

a. The remaining items have all been removed. You won!

b. Only some of them have been removed. Go to **Advanced Credit Repair.**

c. None of them have been removed. Go to **Advanced Credit Repair.**

Basic System for Disputing Four or More Items

You have to get your credit report from each of the credit bureaus, because they're separate reporting agencies, because they often report different things, and because you can't know which report someone is going to use to deny you credit. This means you have to dispute similar items on different credit reports, credit bureau by credit bureau.

Clearing an item off one bureau's report won't clear it off another. (In cases of identity theft, a dispute process initiated at one bureau is supposed to clean up the mess at all three agencies, but it's best not to rely on that. You should dispute even identity theft cases with all three agencies.) The good news is that if you succeed in clearing an item off one report, it's a sign that you'll likely succeed with another credit bureau.

This flowchart is very similar to the flowchart for disputing three or fewer items. Because you never want to dispute more than three items at a time with any one credit bureau (it makes them suspicious that your claim is frivolous), you should only begin with three or so at each bureau. This flowchart is different from the one for three or fewer items, because it shows you how to add new items to the dispute process while you redispute old items.

It's smart to dispute different items with different credit bureaus in order to determine which will most easily be removed from your credit history. For instance, if there are a total of nine bad items on your three credit reports, divide them up into three groups of three and dispute one group with each bureau. Redispute the ones that are removed first with the other bureaus. This across-the-board approach also helps determine which items need **advanced** strategies before wasting a lot of time playing out the **basic** written dispute process. (Even faster: Do the **advanced** disputes that you've identified while the other **basic** written disputes are still going on.) Across-the-board disputes will get you the cleanest credit, most quickly. This is important if you're in a hurry, say, to get a mortgage.

1. Send **initial dispute letter** (page 52). Remember, never dispute more than three items at a time. You'll have a

chance to add more items later in the process, when initial disputes are resolved.

2. Thirty days after Step 1, send the **second-notice letter** (page 55). (The credit bureaus are required by the Fair Credit Reporting Act to respond within 30 days, though they get an additional 15 if you submit additional documentation supporting your claim within that 30-day period.)

3. If, 10 days after Step 2, the credit bureaus still haven't responded, send the **FTC dispute letter** (page 64) with a copy of your **second-notice letter** to both the FTC and the credit bureaus.

4. When you get a response from the credit bureaus, there are three possibilities:
   a. They remove *all* the derogatory items that you disputed. *You've won this round!*
      How to recognize this response. The credit bureaus will send you a letter describing the action they took, plus either a new version of your credit report or an abbreviated version showing the status of any trade lines associated with the dispute. Make sure that the credit bureaus now refer to the disputed credit items as one of the following:

      paid account
      paid as agreed
      current account
      paid satisfactorily
      open/never late
      closed/never late (as long as the account was "closed by consumer"; accounts closed by the creditor are a negative mark)

      On TransUnion's reports, the items that were bracketed or shaded yellow, orange, or red, or different shades of gray, to show a 30-day, 60-day, or 90-

day late payment should now either have no brackets or be green and say "OK."

Note: Make sure that the changed item is now harmless. Sometimes, the credit bureaus will simply change it to a lesser derogatory. (See **Read Your Credit Report** for information on decoding your report.)

What to do next? Send your new disputes, starting again with the **initial dispute letter** (Step 1, above).

b. The second possibility is they remove some but not all of the derogatory items that you disputed. *Don't settle for halfway.*

How to recognize this response. The credit bureaus will send you a letter describing the action they took, plus either a new version of your credit report, or an abbreviated version showing the status of any trade lines associated with the dispute. You'll know what's been corrected, based on the criteria in 4a. Any negative item that has not been corrected will either simply remain on the report, will say "item remains, confirmed by source" or "verified as reported," or the negative item may be changed to a lesser degree of lateness. (See **Read Your Credit Report** for information on decoding your report.)

What to do next? If you're following the across-the-board strategy of disputing different items with different credit bureaus, then play to your success—dispute an item that was removed by one bureau with the others. Hold the items that didn't come off to the side for redisputing later. Following this strategy, you'll go back to the **initial dispute letter** (Step 1) using all new items.

If, however, you have more items to dispute but they are so few (one or two) that you want to redispute the original rejected items immediately, send the **secondary dispute letter** (page 62), in which you will add the one or two new disputes to the original items that weren't removed by your initial dispute.

Or, if you've already successfully disputed at least

three items, and you don't have any more items to add, just items to redispute, send **demand letter 2** (page 59).

c. The third possibility is that the credit bureau corrects none of the items. Don't be frustrated. This is a common result of an inefficient dispute process that puts the entire onus on consumers to prove the items are errors.

How to recognize this response. The credit bureaus will send you an abbreviated credit update or a new full credit report which, next to the disputed items, says "item remains confirmed" or "verified as reported," or the disputed items will simply remain on the report unchanged.

What to do next? If you're following the across-the-board strategy of disputing different items with different credit bureaus, then play to your success—dispute an item that was removed by one bureau with the others. Hold the items that didn't come off to the side for redisputing later. Following this strategy, you'll go back to the **initial dispute letter** (Step 1) using all new items.

If you have more items to dispute but they are so few (one or two) that you want to redispute one or two of the original rejected items immediately, send the **secondary dispute letter,** in which you will add the one or two new disputes to the original items that weren't removed by your initial dispute.

If, however, you have no new items to dispute, send **demand letter 1** to redispute the uncorrected items with stronger language that is rooted in your consumer rights. This works because your more specific complaints force the credit bureau to choose between an expensive investigation and clearing your credit. The credit bureaus have a limited number of roadblocks they're willing to enforce, and if you've gotten to this point, you've already broken through one.

5. When you get a response to a **demand letter** or a **secondary dispute letter** (see Step 4, above), go back to

Step 4 and evaluate your situation. Any item that you do not successfully dispute or redispute should be handled with techniques in the **Advanced Credit Repair** section.

STANDARD CREDIT BUREAU STALLING TECHNIQUES

The law requires that credit bureaus respond to all written disputes. The credit bureaus stall for weeks and months, using the following tricks:

1. They send you a form letter asking you to prove who you are by providing a copy of a utility or phone bill, in addition to Social Security number and current address. Solution: Include this information from the start so you save time.
2. They send you a form letter telling you that your complaint was not specific enough to investigate or correct. Solution: If you carefully follow the step-by-step instructions, your disputes will be clear and legally sound—so you can ignore the delaying tactic and proceed with the next step in the dispute process.
3. They just don't answer. Solution: Send your letters through certified mail from the start. If you haven't got an answer within six weeks, start over, but this time also send a copy of the dispute to the Federal Trade Commission using the **FTC dispute letter** (page 64).

Basic Credit Bureau Disputes: Initial Dispute Letter

Instructions:

1. Write down your name and address with your Social Security number.

2. Write the credit bureau address on the same page (credit bureau addresses are listed in Appendix II).

3. Include a photocopy of two recent bills (phone, electric, etc.) to prove that you are who you are, at your address.

4. Write an opening paragraph to convey the following three points:
   a. There are errors.
   b. The errors are hurting your credit.
   c. The errors will potentially cause you to suffer some specific loss. Each case is different, and so you should, in one or two sentences, say what you personally stand to lose (i.e., a mortgage, an opportunity to buy something, a job because you can't get a car loan).

   Reminder: Dispute no more than three items at a time, and do not treat this as a form letter to be copied word for word. If you do, the credit bureaus may believe that you are using a credit-repair strategy and give you a hard time.

5. Give the name of the creditor that reported bad credit on you, and your account number with that creditor. List each creditor, account number, and dispute separately if you are disputing more than one item.

6. Describe the specific reason why the credit item is wrong. The reason itself will likely never be evaluated, since it's usually too much trouble to sort out your differences with a creditor. Maybe:

   • It's not yours. Have you been confused with someone else? The credit bureaus usually can correct this problem very quickly, because it's so easy for them to check. See the section **If You Suspect the Credit Bureau Is Confusing You With Someone Else** (page 66).
   • There was a billing problem. You were billed at the wrong address, you questioned a bill (you never ordered the merchandise, it wasn't the right item), or a payment wasn't properly credited to your account. The credit bureaus have difficulty evaluating these challenges, and often take your word for it if you are persistent.
   • You're certain that you always paid your account on time, and you can prove it with canceled checks

or some other documentation. The credit bureaus don't ignore proof for very long.

The credit bureaus rarely correct a harmful item if you accept blame for the problem ("I was out of work," "I was sick").

7. Close the letter by signing your name.

8. Send the letter through *certified/return receipt* mail. Otherwise, the credit bureau will know that you don't have legal proof of having sent the letter, and may ignore it.

INITIAL DISPUTE SAMPLE LETTER

The specific reason given in this case for why the item (the Lone Star Bank Corp.) was in error is a blanket denial. See Step 6 in the **Initial Dispute Letter Instructions** for more information.

Your name
Your address
Your phone number
Your Social Security number

Date

Customer Service
Credit bureau name
Credit bureau address

Dear Customer Service:

The following errors are hurting my chances of ever getting a home for my family. If you don't correct them soon, I will lose a $30,000 deposit.

This account is wrong:

LONE STAR BANK CORP.

(Continued)

Account Number 4483847293472394

The Lone Star bank account is not a bad account. Your report says that I was late 60 days twice. I always pay this account on time.

I expect your prompt answer in writing.

Yours,
Joy Q. Public

Basic Credit Bureau Dispute: Second-Notice Letter

Use this letter to follow up your **initial dispute letter** if you get no response after a month.

Instructions:

1. Send a copy of the **initial dispute letter,** either reprinted, rewritten, or photocopied. Include a photocopy of the green postal receipt from your certified letter, or at least note the date you sent the **initial dispute letter.**

2. In your own words, add a notice to the copy that this is the second time you are sending it.

3. Send this letter one month after sending the **initial dispute letter.**

4. Send the letter through *certified/return receipt* mail. Otherwise, the credit bureau will know that you don't have legal proof of having sent the letter, and may ignore it.

SECOND-NOTICE LETTER

Your name
Your address
Your phone number
Your Social Security number

Date

Customer Service
Credit bureau name
Credit bureau address

Dear Customer Service:

What's going on? It's been a month since I sent you the letter below! (A photocopy of my certified-mail receipt is attached.) By law, you must respond within a certain amount of time. I'm counting the days.

The following errors are hurting my chances of ever getting a home for my family. If you don't correct them soon, I will lose a $30,000 deposit.

This account is wrong:

LONE STAR BANK CORP.

Account Number 4483847293472394

The Lone Star bank account is not a bad account. Your report says that I was late 60 days twice. I always pay this account on time.

I expect your prompt answer in writing.

Yours,
Joy Q. Public

Basic Credit Bureau Disputes: Demand Letter 1

This letter is to be used if the credit bureau responds to either your **initial dispute letter** or **second-notice letter** with a refusal to correct *any of the items* on your report. If the credit bureau corrects some items but not others, use **demand letter 2**. If the credit bureau corrected some or all of the items, and you want to dispute more items, use **secondary dispute letter**.

Instructions:

1. Write down your name and address, with your Social Security number.

2. Write the credit bureau address on the same page (credit bureau addresses are listed in Appendix II).

3. Write an opening paragraph to convey the following three points:
   a. They have ignored your complaints of errors on your credit report.
   b. The errors have hurt you financially and continue to do so.
   c. State the ways in which you have been financially penalized for their error. Each case is different, and so you should, in one or two sentences, say what you personally stand to lose (i.e., a mortgage, an opportunity to buy something, a job because you can't get a car loan).

   Reminder: Dispute no more than three items at a time, and do not treat this as a form letter to be copied word for word. If you do, the credit bureaus may recognize that you are using a credit-repair strategy and give you a hard time.

4. Give the name of the creditor that reported bad credit on you, and your account number with that creditor. List each creditor, account number, and dispute separately if you are disputing more than one item.

5. State the specific reason why the credit item is wrong. Use the explanation and logic from the **initial dispute letter.** You may want to go into more detail this time.

6. Explain in your own words that you are going to take stronger action if you don't get satisfaction (i.e., call your lawyer, sue in small claims court, report the credit bureau to the Federal Trade Commission or your state's attorney general).

7. Close the letter by signing your name.

8. Send the letter through *certified/return receipt* mail. Otherwise, the credit bureau will know that you don't have legal proof of having sent the letter, and may ignore it.

DEMAND LETTER 1

Your name
Your address
Your phone number
Your Social Security number

Date

Customer Service
Credit bureau name
Credit bureau address

Dear Customer Service:

I recently wrote you to have an item investigated on my credit report. You claim that you have verified that the item is correct as stated on the report. I don't know how that could be true, since the item is wrong. You seem to have merely repeated the information.

(Continued)

Either correct the problem, or I will take whatever actions are needed to defend myself. This may include holding you responsible for my financial losses.

This account is wrong:

LONE STAR BANK CORP.

Account Number 4483847293472394

The Lone Star bank account is not a bad account. Your report says that I was late 60 days twice. I paid this account on time. Please tell me how I can contact the person who is supplying you with this information.

As I understand the law, you are liable for this error. If you don't correct the mistake immediately, I will take stronger action.

Yours,
Joy Q. Public

Basic Credit Bureau Dispute: Demand Letter 2

This letter is to be used if the credit bureau responds to either your **initial dispute letter** or **second-notice letter** with a refusal to correct *some of the items* on your report. If the credit bureau refuses to correct *any* of the items, use **demand letter 1**. If the credit bureau corrects all or only some of the items, and you want to dispute more items, use the **secondary dispute letter** (page 62).
Instructions:

1. Write down your name and address, with your Social Security number.

2. Write the credit bureau address on the same page (credit bureau addresses are listed in Appendix II).

3. Write an opening paragraph to convey the following three points:
   a. They have ignored your complaints of errors on your credit report.
   b. The errors have hurt you financially and continue to do so.
   c. State the ways in which you have been financially penalized for their error. Each case is different, and so you should, in one or two sentences, say what you personally stand to lose (i.e. a mortgage, an opportunity to buy something, a job because you can't get a car loan).

   Reminder: Dispute no more than three items at a time, and do not treat this as a form letter to be copied word for word. If you do, the credit bureaus may recognize that you are using a credit-repair strategy and give you a hard time.

4. Give the name of the creditor that reported bad credit on you, and your account number with that creditor. List each creditor, account number, and dispute separately if you are disputing more than one item.

5. State the specific reason why the credit item is wrong. Use the explanation and logic from the **initial dispute letter.** You may want to go into more detail this time.

6. Explain in your own words that you are going to take stronger action if you don't get satisfaction (i.e., call your lawyer, sue in small claims court, report the credit bureau to the Federal Trade Commission or your state's attorney general).

7. Close the letter by signing your name.

8. Send the letter through *certified/return receipt* mail. Otherwise, the credit bureau will know that you don't

have legal proof of having sent the letter, and may ignore it.

DEMAND LETTER 2

Your name
Your address
Your phone number
Your Social Security number

Date

Customer Service
Credit bureau name
Credit bureau address

Dear Customer Service:

In the most recent update of my report, I see that you have corrected some of your mistakes, but not all. This isn't a case of some right and some wrong. They were all wrong.

You claim that you have verified the items, but I don't know how that could be true, since they are still in error. You seem to have merely repeated the information.

This account is still wrong:

LONE STAR BANK CORP.

Account Number 4483847293472394

The Lone Star bank account is not a bad account. Your report says that I was late 60 days twice. I paid this account on time. Please tell me how I can contact the person who is supplying you with this information.

(Continued)

As I understand the law, you are liable for this error. If you don't correct the mistake immediately, I will take stronger action.

Yours,
Joy Q. Public

Basic Credit Bureau Dispute: Secondary Dispute Letter

This letter is to be used if the credit bureau responds to either your **initial dispute letter** or **second-notice letter** by correcting some or all of the items, *and you want to dispute more items*. This letter is especially useful if you have many items to dispute and do not want to arouse the suspicions of the credit bureaus by disputing many items all at once.

If the credit bureau refuses to correct any of the items, use **demand letter 1**. If the credit bureau corrects some items, but leave others, use **demand letter 2**.

Instructions:

1. Write down your name and address, with your Social Security number.

2. Write the credit bureau address on the same page (credit bureau addresses are listed in Appendix II).

3. Include a photocopy of two recent bills (phone, electric, etc.) to prove that you are who you are, at your address.

4. Write an opening paragraph to convey the following three points:
    a. You thank them for correcting items, but in your research, you've found some more errors.
    b. The remaining errors are hurting your credit.
    c. State that the errors will potentially cause you to suffer some specific loss. Each case is different, and so you should, in one or two sentences, say what you person-

ally stand to lose (i.e., a mortgage, an opportunity to buy something, a job because you can't get a car loan).

Reminder: Dispute no more than three items at a time, and do not treat this as a form letter to be copied word for word. If you do, the credit bureaus may recognize that you are using a credit-repair strategy and give you a hard time.

5. Give the name of the creditor that reported bad credit on you, and your account number with that creditor. List each creditor, account number, and dispute separately if you are disputing more than one item.

6. State the specific reason why the credit item is wrong. Use the explanation and logic from the **initial dispute letter.** You may want to go into more detail this time.

7. Close the letter by signing your name.

8. Send the letter through *certified/return receipt* mail. Otherwise, the credit bureau will know that you don't have legal proof of having sent the letter, and may ignore it.

SECONDARY DISPUTE LETTER

Your name
Your address
Your phone number
Your Social Security number

Date

Customer Service
Credit bureau name
Credit bureau address

(Continued)

Dear Customer Service:

Your reports are so confusing that I've only now identified another error on my credit report.

The item in error is:

FIRST AMERICA CREDIT CARD

Account Number 47252361293

Your report says that I was 30 days late once, but that's not my fault. That payment was late because I did not receive a bill. The bill was sent to a former address, even though I had notified the company in writing that I moved.

I look forward to a prompt remedy of this unpleasantness.

Yours,
Joy Q. Public

FTC Dispute Letter

This letter is useful if the credit bureaus don't answer your written disputes within six weeks (the 45-day "reasonable time period" that the law gives the credit bureaus to respond).

You are sending this letter so that you can also send a copy to each of the delaying credit bureaus to show that you mean business. Therefore, keep a few copies of this letter for that purpose. (For more information about credit-bureau stalling tactics and credit-repair countermeasures, see **Standard Credit Bureau Stalling Techniques,** page 52.)

FTC DISPUTE LETTER

Your name
Your address
Your phone number
Your Social Security number

Date

Federal Trade Commission
Consumer Response Center
Room 130
600 Pennsylvania Ave. N.W.
Washington, D.C. 20580

Dear Consumer Complaint Dept.:

Credit bureau name won't respond to my complaints about errors in my credit report. Enclosed are a copy of the written dispute and a photocopy of the postal return-receipt card. Please help in any way possible.

Yours truly,
J. Q. Public

You can also send a copy of this to your state's attorney general's office, or your state department of consumer affairs.

Remember, when using this letter and all letters in this book, to:

1. Rephrase the letter in your own words. You don't want to appear as though you are being coached or following a repair strategy.
2. Keep a photocopy of the letter for your records. The copies are often used later in the repair process.
3. Send the letter through *certified/return receipt mail*. This is proof that you sent the letter.

Basic Repair: If You Suspect That the Credit Bureau Is Confusing You with Someone Else

This is the most common and easiest problem to clear up. Send an **initial dispute letter** in which you clearly identify all items that are not yours. This is a special case, in which you can dispute more than three items.

ADVANCED CREDIT REPAIR INTRODUCTION

By this point in the process of repairing your credit rating, you have received and decoded your credit reports from the three major credit bureaus. You have identified the harmful information they are reporting on you, and you are ready to change it.

You may have exhausted the **basic** dispute process, which is essentially a written correspondence with the credit bureaus. Or you may be in a rush, and you want to employ other techniques while the written disputes are running their course. If you're up to it, concurrent **basic** and **advanced** disputes are a good way of expediting the repair process.

The crux of the **advanced** techniques is to understand the creditor who is reporting bad credit on you, and to develop strategies for your particular mix of bad credit items:

- Items best disputed through the basic credit-bureau techniques
- Items best negotiated directly with the creditors
- Knowing when to switch between credit-bureau and creditor negotiations if one method is not working

The following pages will help you plan your repair strategy by assessing the types of creditors you're up against, and which are best suited to direct advanced disputes and which are best handled indirectly through basic disputes with the credit bureaus.

You want to isolate the items that can be negotiated with creditors, because:

- A creditor's agreement to clear an item will clear the item with all three credit bureaus
- The more disputed items you can resolve with the creditors, the easier time you will have with the credit bureaus, which become more resistant when you dispute many separate items simultaneously

Creditors, and the type of credit they give, are the most important factors in planning a strong dispute. There are nine main kinds of creditors and credit, each with its own personality and vulnerabilities, described in the following pages.

Other important factors in choosing a credit bureau or creditor dispute are:

- The age of the item. The credit bureaus often can't confirm older items even when they're true (because the creditors don't keep good archival records).
- The grouped or scattered nature of the latenesses in the payment history. Grouped latenesses are often attributed to one uncredited payment or billing error that caused subsequent payments to appear late.

Creditor Type: Retail Stores

Note: If a retail debt is with a collection agency, also refer to the **Collection Agency** section (page 84).

RETAIL STORE BACKGROUND

The largest department stores are the source of many bad-credit items. Retail credit is an important indicator of how you pay your bills and how you view credit. The stores are aggressive about reporting credit, because they have essentially no leverage in getting you to pay, short of getting a court to force you.

The credit that retailers give you is called "unsecured credit," because they've given you goods, such as clothes, electronics, or furniture, and they really only have your promise that you'll someday give them money.

By reporting any lateness in your payment history, and especially any failure to pay, retailers are usually successful in eventually getting money from deadbeats. As the retailer's reasoning goes, someday the deadbeat will want to buy a house or get a car loan. Then they'll have to pay the outstanding money.

The consistent reporting of latenesses also works to the retailer's advantage. If enough credit customers understand that the late paying will count against them, more people will pay on time. The fear of bad credit gets customers who do pay on time to continue doing so.

RETAIL STORE STRATEGY

With a handful of exceptions, many retailers will clear your credit if you approach them through their customer-service departments and negotiate. Customer-service departments clear credit every day; it's part of their job.

Even if you still owe money, call up customer service and ask plainly to have your credit record restored to good health. Your leverage with the retailers is twofold: They want to be paid, and they want to keep you as a customer.

When you request to have your credit cleared, you may want to tell them that their negative report is preventing you from buying a car or a house. Be insistent. Remind them that you have been a loyal customer, and that you don't want to have to take your business elsewhere because of a simple misunderstanding (always call it a misunderstanding). Work your way up to a supervisor if necessary, and, while keeping your cool, let them hear a hint of the irate customer who could be made happy—if this little credit problem gets straightened out right away.

Retail stores succumb to the wear-'em-down technique more than most creditors. Stick to it even when all seems hopeless, because, as in all credit situations, the system is not set up for people who won't take no for an answer.

You may want to consult **Notes on Retail Store Negotiations** (page 71) to further develop your strategy.

1. Initial negotiation.

   a. If you're up to date in your payments: Make this part of your case with customer service. Some stores will just roll over and say, "Well, you're paid in full, we'll be happy to clear the credit."

Others will say, depending on how bad the credit was, that they won't clear it up—that it's history and you can't change history. This is more likely if you were very delinquent or if the matter proceeded to a lawsuit or judgment against you. If the creditor won't budge, skip to Step 2 below.

b. If you owe money that you are willing to repay: Ask the retailer to clear your credit upon repayment. Include the **"restrictively endorsed" settlement letter** (page 94) with your check, and modify the letter to the specific terms you've negotiated with the retailer.

Note that "restrictively endorsed" letters don't always work. Sometimes the creditor will accept the terms of the letter by cashing the check you've enclosed, but the credit bureaus don't always remove the negative item off your credit report when you send them a copy of the letter. Thus, it's important to follow up with the creditor to ask them to remove the negative item.

c. If you owe more money than you're willing or able to repay immediately, negotiate using the logic of the **"debt schedule" settlement letter** (page 97). You are offering to repay the money according to a strict schedule; you are asking to have your credit cleared, the repayment terms extended, and, possibly, to have the debt reduced.

2. If negotiations don't go well with the customer service departments, you can dictate your own terms to them using the **"restrictively endorsed" settlement letter** (page 94), provided that they cash the check you enclose. You can also use the **"debt schedule" settlement letter** (page 97).

3. Follow up the settlement letter with a letter to the credit bureaus (see **Advanced Credit Bureau Dispute: Documentation Letter,** page 100) to make sure that they ultimately remove the derogatory items you have negotiated off with the creditors.

NOTES ON RETAIL-STORE NEGOTIATIONS

The following negotiating strategies are tailored to retail-reporting disputes involving specific problems with retail-store debt (like credit cards, also known as revolving debt).

Retail stores have layers of customer service. You will most likely reach the person who can help you through an 800 number at a remote site. Unlike almost all other creditors, retail stores will sometimes clear your credit as a matter of simple courtesy. Ask for it first. If customer service says no, it's time to negotiate.

Direct negotiations with retailers work best when:

- You owe money. Offer to pay in exchange for clearing your credit.
- You have irrefutable proof of a creditor error. It could be anything—the couch never came, you didn't order it, etc. The retailer should obviously correct its mistake. You'll still want to follow up with the credit bureaus, since the retailer already proved that it was sloppy.
- There is only one lateness showing. It might not be your fault. The system of crediting and slow mail shouldn't work against you. Everybody deserves a second chance. Don't forget to follow up with the credit bureaus yourself.
- You changed your billing address. You can't be late for not paying what you don't know about, even if the retailer argues otherwise. See **revolving credit—change of billing address letter** (page 103).
- You asked for a bill to be clarified. You can't be late for not paying what you questioned (although you must continue to pay uncontested bills). See **revolving credit—billing clarification letter** (page 101).

Just as you should follow up all successful negotiations with letters to the credit bureaus, you should also follow up unsuccessful negotiations with letters to the credit bureaus. Sometimes clearly stating your side of the story is enough to prompt a credit bureau to remove an item that the creditor still insists on. If the credit bureau doesn't want to pick sides, it will simply drop the item from your report. See **Advanced Credit Bureau Dispute: Documentation Letter** (page 100).

Creditor Type: Banks and Mortgage Lenders

BANK BACKGROUND

Because their business is loaning money, banks aggressively report credit items. The credit-reporting industry was created in large part to aid banks in making lending decisions.

Although banks often grant "secured credit"—meaning that they can attach specific items such as your house or car to a loan agreement—they are still vulnerable to your failure to keep a payment promise.

Credit reporting is an important tool that banks use to ensure they get paid. Banking is also a highly regulated industry. For these reasons, it is difficult to negotiate with a bank. It's much harder for a bank to cut an individual a break, because they are required to treat customers equally.

BANK STRATEGY

Bank negotiations are difficult. Except in cases where you have absolute proof that the bank is in error, you are better off disputing a bad bank-credit item with a credit bureau. Nevertheless, there is some wiggle room for a negotiation.

If you can, build a relationship with an individual who can help you. Polite pestering can get you far with banks, at least to the point where it's easier for them to clear your credit than answer your calls.

Banks sometimes agree to remove bad credit in exchange for payment of past due money, especially if you can demonstrate, to some degree, that there was a problem in the billing. Maybe they weren't notifying you at your correct address or at least the one you asked them to change billing to. Sticking to your story, and couching it in the terms covered later in this book (see **Avoid Ultimatums,** page 100) will go a long way toward getting a bank, or any credit department, for that matter, to see your side and fix the offending credit item.

You may want to consult **Notes on Bank and Mortgage Lender Negotiations** (page 74) in further developing your strategy.

1. Initial negotiation.
   a. If you're fully paid up on the loan, with no remaining payments, forget about disputing with the bank; do a **basic** credit bureau dispute. You will want to include a copy of the **"restrictively endorsed" settlement letter** (page 94) if you included one with your final payment (see **Advanced Credit Bureau Dispute: Documentation Letter,** page 100).
   b. If you owe money that you are willing to repay, ask the bank to clear your credit upon repayment. If they really want the money, they'll cut this deal. Include a **"restrictively endorsed" settlement letter** with your check, and modify the letter to the specific terms you've negotiated with the bank.

      Even if the bank won't agree to clear your credit upon repayment, you can try dictating the terms by enclosing a **"restrictively endorsed" settlement letter** with a payment. Many larger institutions automatically process incoming checks, and thereby agree to your terms by default. Mortgage lenders, and many banks, too, tend to return restrictively endorsed checks. If your check is returned, make your payment without restrictive endorsement right away, to avoid further latenesses, and pursue your dispute with the credit bureaus. The settlement letter can still be useful (see **Advanced Credit Bureau Dispute: Documentation Letter**). But be aware that, even if the bank agrees to the terms of your "restrictively endorsed" settlement letter by cashing your check, that doesn't necessarily mean the credit bureaus will accept a copy of the letter as reason enough to clear the item off your credit report. You may need to follow up with the bank to ask that they clear the item.
   c. If you owe more money than you are able to repay immediately, negotiate using the logic of the **"debt schedule" settlement letter** (page 97). You are offering to repay the money according to a strict schedule; you are asking to have your credit cleared, the repayment terms extended, and possibly to have the

debt reduced. Many banks routinely accept 70-cents-on-the-dollar settlements, but settlements as low as 30 cents on the dollar are possible.

2. Follow up the settlement letter with a letter to the credit bureaus (see **Advanced Credit Bureau Dispute: Documentation Letter,** page 100) to make sure that they ultimately remove the derogatory items you have negotiated off with the creditors.

NOTES ON BANK AND MORTGAGE LENDER NEGOTIATIONS

The following negotiating strategies are tailored to credit-reporting disputes involving specific problems with installment debt. These debts typically involve a coupon book or payment agreement that says you will forgo your right of bill notification before each payment.

Banks, like retail stores, have layers of customer service. The person who can help you will most likely be reached through an 800 number at a remote site. They are different from retailers, though, because they generally won't agree to remove a derogatory credit item just because it's paid or older. For this reason, we don't recommend negotiating by phone with banks.

Direct bank negotiations work best when:

- You have irrefutable proof of a bank error. They should obviously correct their mistake. You'll still want to follow up with the credit bureaus, since the bank already admitted that it was sloppy.
- There's only one lateness showing. It might not be your fault. The system of crediting and slow mail shouldn't work against you. Everybody deserves a second chance. Don't forget to follow up with the credit bureaus yourself.
- There are a number of latenesses showing, but they are all in a row, month after month. You can argue that this is caused by only one uncredited payment, which would cause every payment thereafter to be listed as 30 days late. Because this problem involves a payment lost in the system, you don't have a canceled check or other proof.

This shouldn't stop you from pressing your case. Again, don't forget to follow up with the credit bureaus yourself.

Just as you should follow up all successful negotiations with letters to the credit bureaus, you should also follow up unsuccessful negotiations with letters to the credit bureaus. Sometimes clearly stating your side of the story is enough to prompt a credit bureau to remove an item that the creditor still insists on. If the credit bureau doesn't want to pick sides, it will simply drop the item from your report. See **Advanced Credit Bureau Dispute: Documentation Letter** (page 100).

Creditor Type: Bank-issued and Other Credit Cards (MasterCard/Visa/Discover/American Express)

CREDIT CARD BACKGROUND

Credit card companies, which include banks and other financial services companies, are vulnerable, because the credit they issue is unsecured with other property, money, or merchandise. As such, they are consistent reporters of any lateness or failure to pay.

Bad credit from credit cards mars many credit reports. Credit reporting is an important tool that card companies use to ensure that they get paid. The industry is also highly regulated, and therefore difficult to negotiate with. It's much harder for a credit card lender to cut an individual a break, because it is required to treat customers equally.

The good news is that credit card companies are overburdened. They are often hungry to settle outstanding debts, sometimes for less than the total amount, frequently for the removal of bad credit.

CREDIT CARD STRATEGY

Credit card negotiations are difficult, but the requirement that you be billed accurately and at the address that you state creates some wiggle room. If a bill isn't sent to a correct billing address, or if a consumer seeks to clarify billing amounts, payment cannot be reported as late.

You can learn about the tools at your disposal (see **revolving credit—change of billing address letter,** page 103, and **revolving credit—billing clarification letter,** page 101) now, or follow the negotiation how-to and use them as they are needed.

If you can, build a relationship with an individual who can help you. Polite pestering can get you far with credit card companies, at least to the point where it's easier for them to clear your credit than answer your calls.

Credit card companies sometimes agree to remove bad credit in exchange for payment of past due money, especially if you can demonstrate, to some degree, that there was a problem in the billing. See **Notes on Credit Card Negotiations.**

1. Initial negotiation.
   a. If you're fully paid up on a card account that has been closed but had latenesses, forget about disputing latenesses with the credit card company; do a **basic** credit bureau dispute. You'll want to include a copy of the **"restrictively endorsed" settlement letter** (page 94) if you included one with your final payment (see **Advanced Credit Bureau Dispute: Documentation Letter,** page 100), though you should know that credit-reporting agencies don't always accept "restrictively endorsed" settlement letters as reason enough to delete bad credit items.
   b. If you're willing and able to repay money on an unsettled card account that has been closed and had latenesses, the longer it's been, the more likely they are to clear your credit upon payment, especially if you argue about billing errors (see **Notes on Credit Card Negotiations,** page 77).
   c. If you're not able to repay money on an unsettled card account (open or closed) that had latenesses, negotiate using the logic of the **"debt schedule" settlement letter** (page 97). You are offering to repay the money according to a strict schedule; you are asking to have your credit cleared, the repayment terms extended, and possibly to have the debt reduced.

Many credit card companies routinely accept 70-cents-on-the-dollar settlements, but settlements as low as 30 cents on the dollar are possible.

d. Open accounts: If you're a current customer with late payments on your record but you are able to re-pay the current payment due, send a **"restrictively endorsed" settlement letter** (page 94) with your payment. You are dictating the terms by enclosing a **"restrictively endorsed" settlement letter** with a payment. Many larger institutions automatically process incoming checks, and thereby agree to your terms by default.

Credit card companies rarely return restrictively endorsed checks. If your check is returned, make your payment without restrictive endorsement right away to avoid further latenesses, and pursue your dispute with the credit bureaus. The settlement letter can still be useful (see **Advanced Credit Bureau Dispute: Documentation Letter,** page 100).

2. Follow up the settlement letter with a letter to the credit bureaus (see **Advanced Credit Bureau Dispute: Documentation Letter**) to make sure that they ultimately remove the derogatory items you have negotiated off with the creditors.

NOTES ON CREDIT CARD NEGOTIATIONS

The following negotiating strategies are tailored to credit-reporting disputes involving specific problems with credit card debt (also known as revolving debt).

Credit card companies, like retail stores, have layers of customer service. The person who can help you will most likely be reached through an 800 number at a remote site. They are different from retailers, though, because they won't generally agree to remove a derogatory credit item just because it's paid or it's so old that records are no longer kept—unless you still owe them some money that they don't expect to collect.

Direct negotiations with credit card companies work best when:

- You have irrefutable proof of a credit card company error. They should obviously correct their mistake. You'll still want to follow up with the credit bureaus, since the credit card company already admitted that it was sloppy.
- There's only one lateness showing. It might not be your fault. The system of crediting and slow mail shouldn't work against you. Everybody deserves a second chance. Don't forget to follow up with the credit bureaus yourself.
- You changed your billing address. You can't be late for not paying what you don't know about, even if credit card companies argue otherwise. See **revolving credit—change of billing address letter** (page 103).
- You asked for a bill to be clarified. You can't be late for not paying what you questioned (although you must continue to pay uncontested bills). See **revolving credit—billing clarification letter** (page 101).

Just as you should follow up all successful negotiations with letters to the credit bureaus, you should also follow up unsuccessful negotiations with letters to the credit bureaus. Sometimes clearly stating your side of the story is enough to prompt a credit bureau to remove an item that the creditor still insists on. See **Advanced Credit Bureau Dispute: Documentation Letter,** page 100.

Creditor Type: Auto Loans

AUTO LOAN BACKGROUND
Car lending is unique in the credit world. Because cars are so expensive to stock in inventory and so easy to repossess, car loans are often made to people who might not, for instance, qualify for a mortgage. However, like mortgages, car loans are classified as installment debt. Under most car loan agreements, you are not billed each month for your payment; you are expected to send it in on your own.

Car loan criteria are flexible enough so that people with little or no credit can qualify. Often this involves a cosigner for the young buyer. Another common device is for the dealer to finance the car for you, instead of using a more-rigid bank or major automotive lending institution.

Predictably, this easy sell gives way to heavy collection tactics that include aggressive credit-reporting. Late and missed car payments mar many credit reports and are often the stumbling block to getting more credit.

AUTO LOAN STRATEGY

It's next to impossible to negotiate clean credit from an auto-loan lender, because the lender can always repossess the car if you owe money. (There are some extra considerations discussed in **Notes on auto loan negotiations**.)

Except in cases where you have absolute proof that the lender is in error, you're better off disputing a bad auto-loan credit item (such as "voluntary surrender," "repossession," or latenesses) with a credit bureau (see **Basic Credit Bureau Dispute**).

Because the loan is dead, credit bureaus will sometimes not be able to verify the item, and will be forced to clear it. That said, it's unlikely you'll ever get a "voluntary surrender" or "repossession" removed from your report. If the credit bureau is able to verify the item after repeated disputes as detailed in the **basic** section, exercise your right to have an explanation (no more than 100 words) appended to your credit report. See **Advanced Credit Repair: Sample Explanation Letter** (page 105).

If you have a documented reason why the late marks are wrong, which amounts to absolute proof the lender made an error in crediting your account, or if you were late by a day or so just once or twice, you might prevail in a phone negotiation to get the credit straightened out.

NOTES ON AUTO-LOAN NEGOTIATIONS

Even though it's next to impossible to negotiate with auto-loan lenders, it can still be helpful to know how inflexible they are.

If you miss a payment, you are guilty until proven innocent. Payments sent during the grace period are sometimes recorded as late. Other errors do occur, such as an uncredited payment. You should fight these.

Take care with these people, though. It is especially important to maintain your payments while waiting for an insurance settlement for any car theft or damage issue, even if that settlement is guaranteed. Your agreements with insurance companies are independent of your responsibility to make loan payments. Unlike many other lenders, auto lenders usually refuse to delete bad credit, even if you have documentation (for instance, police and accident reports or repair bills) that the car doesn't work or was stolen.

When planning credit-repair efforts and dealing with auto lenders, expect them to be inflexible. Your best bet is the credit bureaus.

Creditor Type: Student Loan Agencies

Note: If a student loan is with a collection agency, consider skipping to the **Collection Agency** section.

STUDENT LOAN BACKGROUND

Education loans are often guaranteed by the government, although they originate at banks and student loan agencies (depending on what state you live in). Like most bank loans, they are installment loans, which means that you owe a payment whether or not you are billed for it. These are distinguished from most credit-card loan agreements.

Most student-loan agreements allow for forbearance—the right to begin repayment some time in the future (e.g., when you graduate). The rules on when you begin paying back these loans vary with your economic situation, your job status, the time since you've completed school, and any public service that you may have performed.

Typical student-loan problems begin when borrowers don't keep lenders informed that they are still within the scope of the forbearance. You might still be in graduate school, but if you forget to tell the bank, they may list you as having defaulted on your undergraduate loan.

The complex mix of lenders and guarantors often leads to disastrous mistakes when loans are categorized as defaults. One incorrectly defaulted loan becomes many derogatory credit marks as the guarantor takes over and passes the debt to a collection attorney, who in turn gets a court judgment against you. Each step generates its own bad-credit item.

STUDENT-LOAN STRATEGY

The student-loan system is notorious, even in the credit world, for being impossible to work with. Not only is it excruciatingly impersonal, but there are usually many parties involved. Unlike other creditors, even when you get one or more of the lenders/guarantors to agree to correct your credit, they won't necessarily follow through.

The chaotic system can work in your favor, because it makes it extremely difficult for the credit bureaus to confirm information that you dispute and demand to have investigated. Therefore, the most consistently effective strategy is to work at the credit-bureau level. (There are some other considerations, though, discussed in **Notes on Student Loan Negotiations**.) At the same time, stay current with your payment agreement to head off new problems.

Finally, as we noted at the top of this section, if the student loan is in collection, you may want to skip to the **Collection Agency** section. You can also follow these creditor negotiation steps, but include a **"creditor's agreement to clear collection account" letter** (page 95) with any settlement.

1. Initial negotiation.
   a. If the only problem with your student loan (ongoing or fully paid back) is a few latenesses, you can try explaining away the bad marks with the lender (see **Notes on Bank and Mortgage Lender Negotiations,** page 74), but you should also conduct your dispute with the credit bureaus (see Item 2, below).
   b. If your student loan (ongoing or fully paid back) ever went into default, if you have copies of forbearance letters that the lender claims not to have received, you can send them to the lender, but you should also conduct your dispute with the credit bureaus (see Item 2, below).

2. Credit bureau disputes. As explained in the strategy above, you should conduct student loan disputes at the credit bureau level (see **Basic Dispute**). This has the advantage of often getting related bad marks off your reports without having to talk to each party in the student loan chain.

You may also want to see the **Student Loan "Forbearance Notification" Letter** (page 99) and **Advanced Credit Bureau Dispute: Documentation Letter** (page 100) if you have any supporting materials.

NOTES ON STUDENT LOAN NEGOTIATIONS

Student loans have a nasty habit of ending up in court when they're not dealt with. If you have a judgment against you because of your student loan, see **Public Records,** page 87.

Before you are sued, student loans are put into "default" status. This usually means that the loan is taken over by a state or federal student loan agency's collection department. These bureaucratic organizations are lousy at fixing mistakes. Be skeptical about any promise that you do not get in writing. Treat them as an especially dangerous collection agency, because, under the terms of many student loan agreements, they get a judgment against you without notification (see **Public Records** for more about judgments).

Creditor Type: Medical (dental/doctor/lab/hospital)

MEDICAL BACKGROUND

The credit reporting and collection systems associated with health care are just as messed up as the health-care system as a whole. For this reason, medical credit items are included in this book even though they do not, unlike the other creditors discussed, involve some kind of credit agreement. (The negotiation steps below are also useful for dealing with other small creditors who may have handed your account over to a collection agency.)

Slow medical payments do not ordinarily show up on credit reports until the doctor hands the account over to a collection agency or sues. This often happens automatically if the account goes 60 days past due. Thanks to the crazy health-care system, many consumers don't learn of medical bills from third-party providers like labs and specialists until they become collection accounts and damage the consumer's credit.

MEDICAL STRATEGY

When you have a bad debt arising from unpaid health care, you usually have both the collection agency and the doctor to deal with, and possibly a public record.

Most doctors will agree to clear your credit if you pay them the money that you owe (or at least repay the money as part of a repayment schedule). But you will still have to deal with the collection agency if there's one involved. If you don't do anything, the collection agency will probably classify the debt as a "paid collection account," which is bad. It is, therefore, extremely important to discuss and include the **"creditor's agreement to clear collection account" letter** (page 95) as part of any settlement.

1. If you owe money that you are able to pay in a lump sum, ask the doctor to clear your credit upon repayment. Include the **"creditor's agreement to clear collection account" letter** with your check, and modify the letter to the specific terms you've negotiated with the doctor.

2. If you owe more money than you are willing or able to repay immediately, follow the logic of No. 1, but include the logic of the **"debt schedule" settlement letter,** page 97. You are offering to repay the money according to a strict schedule; you are asking to have your credit cleared, the repayment terms extended, and possibly to have the debt reduced. Settlements of 70 cents on the dollar are common, but settlements as low as 30 cents on the dollar are possible. Offers of full payment will expedite the process.

3. If the collection account is already paid, you can ask the creditor to agree to a version of **"creditor's agreement to clear collection account" letter** (take out the part about enclosing a check).

    If that doesn't work, dispute the item through the credit bureaus (see **Basic Dispute**). There are many reasons why an account could be put into collection improperly. Maybe you weren't billed at the right address, or maybe the creditor ignored your requests for clarification of a bill (see **Fair Credit Billing Act,** page 90).

4. Follow up the settlement letter with a letter to the credit bureaus (see **Advanced Credit Bureau Dispute: Documentation Letter,** page 100) to make sure that they ultimately remove the derogatory items you have negotiated off with the creditors.

Creditor Type: Debt Collection Agencies

BACKGROUND

The business of collection agencies is collecting money. They're good at it. The people who work in collections are a distinct subculture with their own lingo and posturing. They talk tough and they push every advantage they have. "Working the client" is the euphemism for a process of intimidation that skirts consumer laws. Phone calls, letters, veiled threats, and even talking to coworkers, family, and neighbors are all collection techniques.

Don't be intimidated by any of this. As with any other debt, you should negotiate the terms of repayment with your needs and rights in mind.

For more background, see **Notes on Collection Agency Negotiations,** page 87.

STRATEGY

1. If you owe money that you are able to pay in a lump sum, try working with the original creditor using the appropriate creditor background section and the **"creditor's agreement to clear collection account" letter,** page 95.

   If that doesn't work, send in the payment to the collection agency as a restrictively endorsed check using a **"restrictively endorsed" settlement letter,** page 94.

   If the collection agency cashes the check, you've won a big part of the battle. Skip to Step 4 below.

   If the collection agency balks at the restrictive endorsement and doesn't deposit the check, they will call. (You included your phone number in the settlement letter.)

Many collection agencies take the position that a legitimate collection account cannot be deleted from your credit reports. They may also say that only the original creditor can decide to have the bad credit removed. These arguments are specious. As a matter of settlement, any item of bad credit can be deleted.

If the collection agency refuses to help clear your credit, there are several approaches that sometimes turn the agency around:

- You can call into question the validity of the original collection action. Maybe you weren't billed at the right address (see **Fair Credit Billing Act,** page 90) or maybe you think you already paid the debt but it was so long ago that you don't have the canceled check. Add "Just to settle the matter, I will pay, but you can't ruin my credit because of this error." Push the argument to a supervisor.
- Demand that the debt be returned to the original creditor for you to work out repayment terms. Use the **cease-communication letter,** page 106.

In the end, they want to be paid, and it doesn't cost them anything to agree to clear your credit. The above explanations give them an excuse to accommodate you.

- If they still won't agree, hire an attorney (see **Appendix X: Using a Lawyer**). A skilled lawyer can often enforce your rights better than you can. Again, collection agencies want to collect money, not fight lawyers. Remember: Although you are willing to pay, you must get your credit cleared in the process. That's your goal.
- If they do agree to your settlement terms, make sure you get the agreement in writing or use your same **"restrictively endorsed" settlement letter** again. Collection agencies tend not to follow up on their promises to clear your credit, so you will want to send this documentation to the credit bureaus once you have it, though you should note that the credit bureaus

don't always delete credit items as a result of a "restrictively endorsed" settlement. You may find that one or two bureaus do respond, and the third doesn't. In that case, you may want to contact an attorney, or get ready to wait. Most credit items can be cleared from your report after 7 years, though bankruptcies are reported for 10 years, and lawsuits and judgments against you can be reported for 7 years or until the statute of limitations runs out, whichever is longer, according to the Federal Trade Commission. Go to Step 3 below.

2. If you owe more money than you are able to repay immediately, first try working a deal with the original creditor using the procedure for that creditor along with the **"creditor's agreement to clear collection account" letter,** page 95. Follow the same logic of Step 1 but include the logic of the **"debt schedule" settlement letter,** page 97. You are offering to repay the money according to a strict schedule; you are asking to have your credit cleared, the repayment terms extended, and possibly to have the debt reduced. Settlements of 70 cents on the dollar are common, but settlements as low as 30 cents on the dollar are possible. Offers of full payment will expedite the process.

3. If the collection account is already paid, you should dispute the item through the credit bureaus (see **Basic Dispute**). Because you don't owe any money that they want, you don't have any leverage with the collection agency. There are many reasons why an account could be put into collection improperly. Maybe you weren't billed at the right address, or maybe the creditor ignored your requests for clarification of a bill (see **Fair Credit Billing Act,** page 90).

4. Follow up the settlement letter with a letter to the credit bureaus (see **Advanced Credit Bureau Dispute: Documentation Letter,** page 100) to make sure that they ultimately remove the derogatory items you have negotiated off with the creditors.

NOTES ON COLLECTION AGENCY NEGOTIATIONS

Don't admit to any wrongdoing, don't merely pay, and don't be threatened. You want the trail of bad credit cleared in exchange for settling the debt. You have leverage, because:

- They want the money.
- You can control the way in which they contact you (see **Fair Debt Collection Practices Act,** Appendix VI).
- You can refuse to deal with the collection agency (see **cease-communication letter,** page 106), which, as a matter of course, causes the debt to revert back to the original creditor.

The first rule of dealing with collection agencies is *don't be intimidated.* They will often threaten to ruin your credit, not to mention your life. The law, however, regulates what they can and can't do (see **Fair Debt Collection Practices Act**).

Also, with your credit score in mind, make sure the collector doesn't update an old account with a new date simply because you make payment. Credit score risk models look much more unfavorably on recent bills that went unpaid than on past-due accounts that are years old. If the collection agency reports your newly-paid-but-old account as a new item, that sets the clock ticking again on what's considered a negative entry even though you've paid it off. Get the collector to promise to keep reporting the original "date of last activity" before handing over your money.

Finally, unless your original agreement with the creditor provided for special collection fees, the collection agency cannot tack on extra fees for their "service." Don't fall for this common trick.

Creditor Type: Public Records

PUBLIC RECORDS BACKGROUND

Any conviction, court suit, judgment, or tax lien is a matter of public record that may be picked up and reported by the credit bureaus.

Even if you believe that the suit or judgment is unjustified, and can get the other side of the case to agree with you, the credit bureaus have taken the position that what occurred, however unjustified, is history and therefore in the realm of their reporting.

The credit bureaus collect public records in huge gulps of electronic data gathered by subcontractors who compile the records for sale. These companies are notorious for their carelessness. In one celebrated instance, the taxpayers of an entire Vermont town were reported as having tax liens. The shoddy means by which public records are compiled are equaled only by the quality of credit bureau efforts to verify the information when challenged. Much to the dismay of lenders and other people who depend on credit reports, credit bureaus sometimes don't even bother to confirm information that is disputed even when substantiation is readily available.

PUBLIC RECORDS STRATEGY

The two dispute paths depend on whether or not you actually owe money.

If the derogatory public record involves a situation where you owe money, you can try to cut a deal with the creditor or creditor's attorney. In order to vacate a judgment, you will likely need the help of an attorney (see **Appendix X: Using a Lawyer**), especially if you are facing a collection attorney. A thorough collection attorney can eventually get a marshal to enforce collection of the debt. This can involve seizure and sale of your worldly possessions.

If you still owe the money on a judgment filed by a private individual or concern, you might persuade the opposing attorney to vacate the judgment in exchange for payment. Do not confuse this with satisfying the judgment, which only means that you paid when you were forced to. Vacating the judgment means that the judgment has been found defective in some way or that, at least, the opposition feels that the judgment is sufficiently unenforceable that they are willing to settle the matter rather than further pursue the issue with you in court.

Judges have shown a dislike for vacating judgments that were made based on the facts. They are more comfortable with having them satisfied. Still, your attorney can work to have the opposing attorney see the wisdom of accepting payment in exchange for a letter that shows her willingness to have the judgment vacated. The phrase "this judgment may be vacated without prior notice by either party" may be useful to your lawyer in the settlement. The written settlement should always be sent to the credit bureaus (see **Advanced Credit Bureau Dispute: Documentation Letter,** page 100) to make sure that they remove the item.

If the derogatory public record in dispute is not current, your best bet is to work through the credit bureaus. When conducting your **basic** dispute, keep in mind that erroneous public records that don't come off in the first round often come off in the second.

Any accurate information related to a bankruptcy can stay on your report up to 10 years, while information about a lawsuit or judgment against you can be reported for 7 years or until the statute of limitations runs out, whichever is longer.

NOTES ON VERBAL NEGOTIATIONS

Creditors' collection agents are generally aggressive, demeaning, and capable of doing and saying anything to get you to pay. Respect has little to do with their job. Fortunately for you, the law generally gives a second chance to pay up, and creditors are restrained to some extent from unfair debt-collection practices. Professional credit departments for most credit-granting organizations are staffed with individuals who are trained with finely honed rhetorical weapons, designed to instill the guilt and fear that will motivate payment.

Don't make your arguments personal

Focus on the facts of your case, and never get angry at the person representing the other side. Say, "I know you're just doing your job." The people you're dealing with are likely following policy, and to the limited extent that they can influence policy, you are best placed in their good graces. Many, many credit situations involve the person on the other side deciding at his or her own discretion to give you some slack. This is a prime consideration when calling on the phone to get bad credit removed. Statements that are likely to help:

"I realize that this isn't your doing, and that you have a job with responsibilities. Here's the problem. The bad-credit mark from your company that is on my credit report is the only thing that is stopping the mortgage from going through (the baby from getting a crib; my mother from having a last vacation . . . she's very sick). Could you please, please, please help me with this? I'm a paying customer, and I'm going to continue doing business with you, so please help me out here."

The person you are dealing with is elevated, and the problem is reduced to basic life issues. Your position is easy to understand and easy to go along with.

Avoid ultimatums

Instead of saying "I want you to fix my credit—or else," try "I am interested in resolving this credit problem and I need your help. I will satisfy you in whatever reasonable manner necessary to get this problem resolved."

You might offer up some possible reasons why the item was not really late, or that there was a misunderstanding. They might be willing to offer a payment schedule in exchange for clearing the credit. If there were irregularities, or if you can express your claim of problems in a convincing manner, they may just go along with you whether they agree with your claims or not.

The **Fair Credit Billing Act** and the **Fair Credit Reporting Act** have provisions that detail the rules for what is an on-time payment and what is a correct billing procedure. The existence of billing errors, which would mean you weren't really late, will allow the creditor—that is, the creditor's agent in the collections department—to erase the credit.

These requirements for proper billing can be used to shift the burden of proof to the creditor. The other side will, in many instances, cave in rather than fight, whether they believe you or not.

An example of an error we've seen claimed that resulted in the clearing of credit is:

"The bills were sent to my address while construction work was going on. We requested that the bills be sent to my job. It was only after the work was done and we moved back home that we found your bill. Of course, we paid when we knew about it."

This situation, executed as a good-natured cajoling, goes a long way in the credit-reporting world, especially if the past-due accounts have been brought up to date, or the latenesses are older.

If the other side still won't budge

You must offer a number of options on how the problem can be resolved, including a plan the creditor may have in mind, and then choose one.

Offering several possible solutions allows both sides to bring more to the table than was originally in discussion. For example, the original creditor requests that you start making payments to bring the account at least out of collection. This request could be negotiated by you to a larger initial payment, and the promise of accelerated pay-down of the debt in exchange for cleared credit.

When you negotiate a payment plan, admit no guilt, and assign no blame to the other party. Just stick to the misunderstanding. ("The bills weren't coming to me because of construction. I notified you. We obviously didn't communicate well with each other, but I'd like to rectify this now by paying you. Please don't penalize me by ruining my credit.")

When dealing with credit departments, keep it real. Don't insult anyone's intelligence with outlandish fakery. Keep it simple and stick to your explanation. Again, your goal is to get your credit cleared.

Don't give up

Often, repetitive claims of a misunderstanding coupled with your willingness to pay, driven home to each successive layer of entrenched bureaucracy in the credit department, all the way from the customer service rep to the supervisor to the manager to the manager's vice president, gets the job done.

In moving from customer service rep up the line to the vice president, remember to focus on the problem, not pick on the people:

"I understand it's your job to say no to people like me when the issues are not cut-and-dry. You must understand that—except for this misunderstanding, which I've tried to explain—I pay my accounts, and I can't accept no for an answer. Please, may I speak to a supervisor? By the way, what's your name? I wanted to thank you for listening to my problem, even if you couldn't help out. And what's your supervisor's name? Do they have a direct-dial number over there, just in case we get cut off?"

Listen to the person's tone

In credit departments, especially in better-managed companies, the first layer of customer service is supposed to take care of the problem. If they can't, it reflects poorly on them. The higher you go, the more poorly it reflects on the lower levels of customer service.

The negotiation is going your way when someone answers your request to speak to the next level with a strained, "I don't know what good it will do you." In general, moving up the ladder means overcoming obstacles to success. The more strain this request causes, the more likely you will succeed at the next level. When the strain is palpable, repeat some formulation of your original offer to pay, or maybe even your willingness to just go away if you're already paid, in exchange for clear credit. Restate the original misunderstanding in human terms.

Get agreements in writing

Most companies will send you a letter verifying that they are correcting the credit and notifying the credit bureaus. You'll need this letter for your own disputes with the credit bureaus (see **Advanced Credit Bureau Dispute: Documentation Letter,** page 100), in addition to securing your agreement with the creditor.

Advanced: Residential Mortgage Credit Report

In the preparation of a mortgage application, two or three credit-bureau reports are combined as the basis of what is known as a **Residential Mortgage Credit Report** (formerly a **Full Factual Credit Report**). These reports are prepared by a number of credit-reporting companies that are essentially subcontractors to the three major credit bureaus. They function as service companies to the mortgage industry.

For a fee of $55 to $65 (some mortgage lenders absorb this cost), these mortgage-reporting companies go beyond the work of a credit bureau and actually make phone calls (among other verification methods) to make a more informed judgment about your creditworthiness. They verify your employment, salary, address, and—here's the good part—are obligated to issue a corrected credit report if you provide them with evidence of errors in your credit history. The advantage is that the corrected credit report is issued in days, not the weeks and months that the credit bureaus can take. That cleaning up of your credit report can mean thousands of dollars in savings over the life of your mortgage loan. The disadvantage is that the corrections are not necessarily disseminated nationally, so you may still have to go through a repair process with the credit bureaus.

This is really only useful if you're applying for a mortgage. Unfortunately, credit bureaus will only rarely accept a clean Residential Mortgage Credit Report as a basis for removing derogatory items. The shame is that the Residential Mortgage Credit Report is the only report in the credit-reporting business that allows for your corrections to be quickly investigated and processed.

If you apply for a mortgage, the mortgage broker or lending institution will take down basic financial and personal information, which they will then forward to a regional credit report reseller to investigate your creditworthiness.

If there are any derogatory items in your credit report, you'll get a letter from your potential lender asking you to verify their accuracy and explain the circumstances of them.

If the reseller provides your lender a supplementary report with corrections, it will help your mortgage rate, but it may not effect change in the records the national agencies hold on you. For an extra fee, though, some mortgage lenders will ask the credit-agency reseller to perform a "rapid rescore," whereby inaccurate information on a report is disputed through a fast-track process at the credit bureau that published the information—and that means removal of the errors on your report. Not all mortgage lenders offer rapid rescoring, but when they do, it can mean an improved credit report in just days.

The downside is, while some lenders absorb the fee, others don't, and it's steep: About $30 to $45 per item per agency.

You should be as simple as possible in your disputes, relying on straightforward explanations and/or supporting documents (i.e. bills, canceled checks, receipts). Follow the format of the **initial dispute letter** used for the credit bureaus. This process is set up to quickly correct errors that would kill a mortgage deal, and it takes place on a more personal level than your typical disputes with the credit bureaus.

Sometimes one of these small credit-reporting agencies will take the position that disputes should only be conducted with the major credit bureaus, but under the law (see **Fair Credit Reporting Act**, Appendix V), they are a "credit-reporting agency" with the same responsibilities as a credit bureau. You may need to firmly remind a supervisor of this fact when asking the agency to fix errors.

Creditor's "Restrictively Endorsed" Settlement Letter

This method uses what's known as a restrictively endorsed payment and a return receipt, to create a legal agreement between you and a creditor. Your terms become an agreement when the creditor cashes your check. Even if the creditor doesn't honor your call for clearing your credit, the credit bureaus might (see **Advanced Credit Bureau Dispute: Documentation Letter,** page 100). This is a common way for businesses to get consumers' tacit agreement. The telephone companies are perhaps the best examples: You cash this $10 or $25 check, and that signals that you want to switch providers. But some creditors, such as mortgage lenders, will not accept restrictively endorsed payment instruments. And there's no guarantee credit bureaus will accept a copy of such a letter and a cashed check as evidence that negative credit items should be removed. But sometimes one or two of the agencies will respond to such letters, so it's worth a try.

The restrictively endorsed payment can be combined with a **"debt schedule" settlement letter,** page 97.

LETTER

Creditor name
Creditor address*
Creditor phone
Date

*It is important to use the correct address. Although there may be more than one address, the one for "billing inquiries" is the one you should use.

(Continued)

> Dear Customer Service:
>
> Enclosed please find payment for my charge account. Your acceptance of the check signifies that the account is [paid in full or paid up to date] and that you will delete all derogatory items with all the major credit bureaus.
>
> Thank you. I want to extend my thanks to the customer service department for being so helpful with this misunderstanding.
>
> Yours truly,
> J. Q. Public

Remember, when using this letter and all letters in this book, to:

1. Rephrase the letter in your own words. You don't want to appear like you are being coached or following a repair strategy.
2. Keep a photocopy of the letter for your records. The copies are often used later on in the repair process.
3. Send the letter through *certified/return receipt* mail. This is proof that you sent the letter.

"Creditor's Agreement to Clear Collection Account" Letter

This letter is useful for creditors who do not report to credit bureaus, but who refer past-due accounts to collection agencies. The collection agencies, it should come as no surprise, are active credit bureau reporters (see **Creditor Type: Collection Agencies,** page 84, for more detail).

The purpose of the letter is to get the creditor to call off the collection agency. If you do not do it correctly, the collection agency will merely report your late account as "paid collection account," which is still a bad mark on your credit report.

You don't need this letter if the collection agency agrees to clear the bad credit, but that is ordinarily more difficult to achieve than getting a creditor to agree to this letter. Many small-time creditors, like doctors or local hardware stores, are surprised when they find how unhelpful their collection agencies are, and you sometimes have to open their eyes to the problem. This letter gets it in writing so that even if the creditor doesn't follow through, you still have proof of the agreement for the credit bureaus (see **Advanced Credit Bureau Dispute: Documentation Letter,** page 100).

The word "misunderstanding" is an effective way to characterize the collection situation without admitting or assigning blame.

The agreement can be combined with a **"debt schedule" settlement letter,** page 97.

LETTER

Creditor name
Creditor address*
Creditor phone
Date

*It is important to use the correct address. Although there may be more than one address, the one for "billing inquiries" is the one you should use.

Dear [use the contact's name]:

I am glad that we are able to settle our misunderstanding. Enclosed please find [full, or if you're using a repayment schedule, the first installment] payment. Your acceptance of the check signifies that the account is [paid in full or paid up to date] and that you will contact the relevant credit bureaus and collection agencies to delete any collection accounts or other derogatory credit.

I appreciate your cooperation and service. Thank you.

Best regards,
J. Q. Public

Remember, when using this letter and all letters in this book, to:

1. Rephrase the letter in your own words. You don't want to appear like you are being coached or following a re-pair strategy.
2. Keep a photocopy of the letter for your records. The copies are often used later on in the repair process.
3. Send the letter through *certified/return receipt* mail. This is proof that you sent the letter.

Creditor "Debt Schedule" Settlement Letter

Use this letter (or a variation, depending on your circumstances) when you negotiate to repay a debt through regular payments. The repayment terms can vary widely, but the basic point is that you want your credit cleared as soon as you start paying the money back.

Lump sums are the most likely to induce a creditor to accept your offer of partial payment. Still, since debt counselors commonly use 40-month repayment plans, and Chapter 13 bankruptcy often involves 60-month repayment plans, an offer of payment in 12 to 24 months will be relatively fast. Keeping the plan under a year is the next best thing to a lump sum.

LETTER

Creditor name
*Creditor address**
Creditor phone
Date

*It is important to use the correct address. Although there may be more than one address, the one for "billing inquiries" is the one you should use.

(Continued)

Dear Customer Service:

Due to severe financial and health problems in my family, I find it necessary to settle my debts as best I can.

With this letter, I offer to settle my outstanding debt to you for 30 percent of its total amount. In other words, I am offering you $___to be paid in___monthly payments of $___. As long as I stick to these payment terms, you agree to delete all derogatory credit and report this account as current and satisfactory.

If this is agreeable to you, please sign and date below and return to me.

Thank you. I want to extend my thanks to the customer service department for being so helpful with this misunderstanding.

Yours truly,   _____
J. Q. Public   creditor name and date

Remember, when using this letter and all letters in this book, to:

1. Rephrase the letter in your own words. You don't want to appear like you are being coached or following a repair strategy.
2. Keep a photocopy of the letter for your records. The copies are often used later on in the repair process.
3. Send the letter through *certified/return receipt* mail. This is proof that you sent the letter.

Student Loan "Forbearance Notification" Letter

Student loans that leave repayment until after graduation require the borrower to notify all lenders about school enrollment or other circumstances that allow a forbearance on repayment of the loan. If the lender pushes your loan into default, you will want to show the credit bureaus that you served the lender with a forbearance letter (see **Advanced Credit Bureau Dispute: Documentation Letter,** page 100).

LETTER

Student loan lender name
Student loan lender address*
Student loan lender phone
Date
*It is important to use the correct address, which you will find on the loan agreement itself. Many lenders have more than one address, and use a different address for each of their various loan products.

Dear Customer Service:

Please consider this formal notification that I am still in school, and therefore the terms of the forbearance of my student loan are still in effect. I will notify you when I have graduated—and the subsequent grace period has elapsed—by sending you a check for the first payment on the loan.

Thank you.

Yours truly,
J. Q. Public

Remember, when using this letter and all letters in this book, to:

1. Rephrase the letter in your own words. You don't want to appear like you are being coached or following a repair strategy.
2. Keep a photocopy of the letter for your records. The copies are often used later on in the repair process.
3. Send the letter through *certified/return receipt* mail. This is proof that you sent the letter.

Advanced Credit Bureau Dispute: Documentation Letter

Use this letter as a followup to an unresolved dispute with a creditor. Its purpose is to prompt the credit bureau to remove derogatory items that the creditor may not have corrected. You can send any documentation with this letter—the more the better—but the following settlement letters are especially effective, because they substantiate an agreement between you and the creditor: "**restrictively endorsed**," "**debt schedule**," and **student loan** "**forbearance notification**" letters. Also include, with all documentation, photocopies of postal return receipts and canceled checks whenever possible. It is unethical to send copies of the above letters to credit bureaus if you never actually sent them to creditors, but anecdotal evidence suggests that credit bureaus don't generally investigate the validity of consumer-supplied documentation.

LETTER

Creditor name
*Creditor address**
Creditor phone
Date

*It is important to use the correct address. Though there may be more than one address, the one for "billing inquiries" is the one you should use.

(Continued)

Dear Customer Service:

The following error is still on my report despite the fact that I have documentation (enclosed) that demonstrates that this should no longer be reported as bad credit. I would not press such a minor matter if the consequences weren't so severe. I stand to lose money if this is not corrected posthaste.

LONE STAR BANK CORP. account number 4483847293472394.

The enclosed documentation proves that this should be corrected to reflect my good credit.

Yours truly,
J. Q. Public

Remember, when using this letter and all letters in this book, to:

1. Rephrase the letter in your own words. You don't want to appear like you are being coached or following a repair strategy.
2. Keep a photocopy of the letter for your records. The copies are often used later on in the repair process.
3. Send the letter through *certified/return receipt* mail. This is proof that you sent the letter.

Revolving Credit: Billing Clarification Letter

Many of your rights as a revolving-credit borrower derive from the Fair Credit Billing Act (see **Appendix VII**). Revolving credit is the technical name for a credit card or department-store account. It revolves because you can borrow and pay on a monthly basis, with a credit ceiling and a minimum payment. It is distinguished from an installment loan (typically a mortgage, student, or car loan) that has a predetermined monthly payment.

This letter sets the stage for invoking some of your most robust rights under the Fair Credit Billing Act. The act requires revolving-credit lenders to bill you accurately, and at the address that you state, on a monthly basis.

This means that your payment is not late if, within two billing cycles, you send in a request for clarification of amounts due. Under the Fair Credit Billing Act, this request for clarification is classified as a billing error. The payment cannot, therefore, be reported as "late."

With return-receipt proof of having mailed this clarification letter, you can demand that affected lateness on your credit report be corrected. Even without return-receipt proof, sending a copy of the letter is often enough to get either the creditor or credit bureau to correct latenesses (see **Advanced Credit Bureau Dispute: Documentation Letter,** page 100).

LETTER

Creditor name
*Creditor address**
Creditor phone
Date

*It is important to use the correct address. Though there may be more than one address, the one for "billing inquiries" is the one you should use.

Dear Customer Service:

On my latest bill [be specific about card number and billing date], I am confused by the amount owing. I am not sure whether one of the charges is correct. [List the charge.]

Since I am writing you within 60 days of the actual charge, I request that you not report this specific payment as late.

(Continued)

Thank you. I want to extend my thanks to the customer service department for being so helpful with this misunderstanding.

Yours truly,
J. Q. Public

Remember when using this letter, and all letters in this book, to:

1. Rephrase the letter in your own words. You don't want to appear like you are being coached or following a repair strategy.
2. Keep a photocopy of the letter for your records. The copies are often used later on in the repair process.
3. Send the letter through *certified/return receipt* mail. This is proof that you sent the letter.

Revolving Credit: Change of Billing Address Letter

Many of your rights as a revolving-credit borrower derive from the Fair Credit Billing Act (see **Appendix VII**). Revolving credit is the technical name for a credit card or department-store account. It revolves, because you can borrow and pay on a monthly basis, with a credit ceiling and a minimum payment. It is distinguished from an installment loan (typically a mortgage, student, or car loan) that has a predetermined monthly payment.

This letter sets the stage for invoking some of your most robust rights under the Fair Credit Billing Act. The act requires revolving-credit lenders to bill you accurately, and at the address that you state, on a monthly basis.

This means that 20 days before the end of any billing cycle, you can change your billing address. If the creditor does not bill you at the new address that you specify, then you haven't been billed, and you therefore can't be late with payment.

(You can also use the "change of address form" if one came with the bill.)

With return-receipt proof of having mailed this change-of-address letter, you can demand that affected latenesses on your credit report be corrected. Even without return-receipt proof, sending a copy of such a letter is often enough to get either the creditor or credit bureau to correct latenesses (see **Advanced Credit Bureau Dispute: Documentation Letter,** page 100).

Customer service departments will often counter the exercise of your Fair Credit Billing Act rights with specious arguments, such as: "If you charged it, you should have known about it"; "We don't have to bill you, it's just a courtesy"; "The bill wasn't returned, so it must have been received." Don't be intimidated by these arguments.

LETTER

Creditor name
Creditor address*
Creditor phone
Date

*It is important to use the correct address. Though there may be more than one address, the one for "billing inquiries" is the one you should use.

Dear Customer Service:

Consider this letter formal notice of a change in my billing address for my account with you [be specific about card number].

Thank you. I am a satisfied and loyal customer.

Yours truly,
J. Q. Public

Remember, when using this letter and all letters in this book, to:

1. Rephrase the letter in your own words. You don't want to appear like you are being coached or following a repair strategy.
2. Keep a photocopy of the letter for your records. The copies are often used later on in the repair process.
3. Send the letter through *certified/return receipt* mail. This is proof that you sent the letter.

Advanced Credit Repair: Sample Explanation Letter

The Fair Credit Reporting Act requires the credit bureaus to include, at your request, a statement from you of up to 100 words explaining each and any derogatory credit item.

This is a last-ditch technique, after you've given up. It's not really a repair tactic, because it doesn't improve your credit. Nevertheless, in hopeless cases such as car repossessions, it's still better than nothing. Just the fact that you bothered to include an explanation can demonstrate a certain reliability on your part.

In composing your explanation, do not assign blame. Show how you have taken responsibility for your life and the problems you faced. This sample concerns a "voluntary surrender" item listed on a car loan.

LETTER

Credit bureau name
Credit bureau address
Date

Dear Sir or Madam:

Please append the explanation below to my credit report with regard to the following account:

Ford Credit 23456789

(Continued)

At the end of 1989, downsizing in my industry led to massive layoffs. When I lost my job, I could not continue making car payments so I voluntarily surrendered the car.

I took the layoff as an opportunity to be retrained for the position I now have with my present employer. Now that I am working again, I am pleased to be current with all my credit accounts. Credit is very important to me; I regard it as keeping my word.

Thank you. Please send me a copy of the amended credit report.

Yours truly,
J. Q. Public

Remember, when using this letter and all letters in this book, to:

1. Rephrase the letter in your own words. You don't want to appear like you are being coached or following a repair strategy.
2. Keep a photocopy of the letter for your records. The copies are often used later on in the repair process.
3. Send the letter through *certified/return receipt* mail. This is proof that you sent the letter.

Advanced Credit Repair: Cease Communication Letter

This letter is useful if a collection agency won't negotiate or accept a restrictively endorsed payment. After receiving the letter, the collection agency is allowed only one last chance to contact you, and then only to tell you what will happen next.

In effect, this letter cuts the collection agency off at the knees. The agency may return the debt to the original creditor, who should be more willing to negotiate, but you can still call up the collection agency and press your offer one last time before the collection agency gives up the debt (and chance to profit).

While this letter will force the collector to stop contacting you, it won't get rid of any debt you might owe.

LETTER

Collection agency name
Collection agency address
Date

Dear Sir or Madam:

Please cease communication with me in regard to *creditor name, account numbers, and debt.* If you do not abide by this request, you will be in violation of the Fair Debt Collection Practices Act.

Yours truly,
J. Q. Public

Remember, when using this letter and all letters in this book, to:

1. Rephrase the letter in your own words. You don't want to appear like you are being coached or following a repair strategy.
2. Keep a photocopy of the letter for your records. The copies are often used later on in the repair process.
3. Send the letter through *certified/return receipt mail.* This is proof that you sent the letter.

Appendixes

Appendix I

CREDIT BUREAU CONTACT INFORMATION FOR REQUESTING CREDIT REPORTS

Thanks to the Fair and Accurate Credit Transactions Act of 2003, consumers can now get one free report from each of the three credit bureaus each year. To order your free annual credit report online, go to Annualcreditreport.com.

To order by phone, call 877-322-8228.

Consumers can also get their free reports by completing the Annual Credit Report Request Form located on page 12 of this book or online at http://www.ftc.gov/credit, under "free annual reports." Then mail the form to Annual Credit Report Request Service, P. O. Box 105281, Atlanta, GA 30348-5281.

If you've exhausted the free options, you can order your credit report from each of the three main credit-reporting agencies, and the most they can charge you is $9.50. When you order, you'll need to provide your name, address, Social Security number, and date of birth. To verify your identity, the bureaus require you to provide some information that only you would know, like former addresses, the amount of your monthly mortgage payment, or the name of the bank holding your student loans.

EQUIFAX

To order from the Web site, go to Equifax.com. To find the cheapest report, look for "Equifax Credit Report" under the "Other Products" heading.

To order your Equifax report by phone, call 800-685-1111.

To order your Equifax report through the mail:

Equifax Credit Information Services
P. O. Box 740241
Atlanta, GA 30374

TRANSUNION

To order from the Web site, go to Transunion.com. To find the cheapest basic report, look under "Other Credit Report Options."

To order your TransUnion report by phone, call 800-916-8800.

To order it through the mail:
TransUnion
P. O. Box 2000
Chester, PA 19022

EXPERIAN

To order from the Web site, go to Experian.com. To find the cheapest basic report, click on "Experian Credit Report."

To order your Experian report by phone, call 888-397-3742.

Experian
P. O. Box 2104
Allen, TX 75013

Appendix II

CREDIT BUREAU CONTACT INFORMATION FOR FILING DISPUTES

Each of the agency Web sites offers an online dispute option.
http://www.experian.com/disputes
http://www.transunion.com/investigate
http://www.investigate.equifax.com

Because the credit bureaus use a variety of addresses and phone numbers, it's best to use the address and phone number given on your credit report for disputes or investigations. Also, the bureaus usually provide a dispute form with your credit report (for instance, Equifax calls it a "research request") that's preprinted with some of your information.

Appendix III

REPORTING IDENTITY THEFT TO THE CONSUMER REPORTING AGENCIES

If you suspect you've been a victim of identity theft, let the CRAs know immediately. You can very easily place, with a phone call or online, an initial fraud alert that will stay for 90 days on your report. You'll need to provide the basic information: name, Social Security number, and address. Filing an initial fraud alert gives you access to a free credit report from each of the agencies.

A longer-term fraud alert requires you to provide to the agencies a copy of an identity theft report that you filed with a law enforcement agency. This alert lasts for up to 7 years, and includes two additional free credit reports over the ensuing 12 months. Go to the FTC's Identity Theft section for more information: http://www.ftc.gov/credit.

To place a fraud alert on your credit report through Equifax, call 800-525-6285.

To mail documentation to verify the fraud, write to:

Equifax Credit Information Services
Consumer Fraud Division
P. O. Box 740256
Atlanta, GA 30374

To place a fraud alert on your credit report through TransUnion, call 800-680-7289.

To mail documentation verifying the fraud, write to:

TransUnion
Fraud Victim Assistance Department
P. O. Box 6790
Fullerton, CA 92834

To place a fraud alert on your credit report through Experian, call 888-397-3742.

To mail documentation verifying the fraud, write to:

Experian
P. O. Box 9556
Allen, TX 75013

Appendix IV

FILING A COMPLAINT WITH THE FEDERAL TRADE COMMISSION

To file a complaint about problems with a credit-reporting agency, contact the FTC:

Federal Trade Commission
Consumer Response Center, Room 130
600 Pennsylvania Ave., NW
Washington, DC 20580
Or call the FTC: 877-382-4357
Or go to FTC.gov and click on "file a complaint."

Appendix V

FAIR CREDIT REPORTING ACT (INCLUDING FAIR AND ACCURATE CREDIT TRANSACTIONS ACT AMENDMENTS)

The FCRA provides the basic tools for credit repair, and the FACT Act amendments provide for some of the new consumer protections described in this updated *Guerrilla Guide to Credit Repair*. The repair section makes extensive use of the act. It may help to read the actual law, included here in part for you. For the full statute, go to http://www. ftc.gov/os/statutes/050131fcra.pdf. (Note that portions of the FACT Act have different effective dates and are being phased in over time, as the FTC and the Federal Reserve Board write specific regulations.)

§602. Congressional findings and statement of purpose [15 U.S.C. § 1681]

(a) *Accuracy and fairness of credit reporting*. The Congress makes the following findings:

(1) The banking system is dependent upon fair and accurate credit reporting. Inaccurate credit reports directly impair the efficiency of the banking system, and unfair credit reporting methods undermine the public confidence which is essential to the continued functioning of the banking system.

(2) An elaborate mechanism has been developed for investigating and evaluating the credit worthiness, credit standing, credit capacity, character, and general reputation of consumers.

(3) Consumer reporting agencies have assumed a vital role in assembling and evaluating consumer credit and other information on consumers.

(4) There is a need to insure that consumer reporting agencies exercise their grave responsibilities with fairness, impartiality, and a respect for the consumer's right to privacy.

(b) *Reasonable procedures*. It is the purpose of this title to require that consumer reporting agencies adopt reasonable procedures for meeting the needs of commerce for consumer credit, personnel, insurance, and other information in a manner which is fair and equitable to the consumer, with regard to the confidentiality, accuracy, relevancy, and proper utilization of such information in accordance with the requirements of this title.

§ 603. Definitions; rules of construction [15 U.S.C. § 1681a]

(a) Definitions and rules of construction set forth in this section are applicable for the purposes of this title.

(b) The term "person" means any individual, partnership, corporation, trust, estate, cooperative, association, government or governmental subdivision or agency, or other entity.

(c) The term "consumer" means an individual.

(d) Consumer Report

(1) *In general.* The term "consumer report" means any written, oral, or other communication of any information by a consumer reporting agency bearing on a consumer's credit worthiness, credit standing, credit capacity, character, general reputation, personal characteristics, or mode of living which is used or expected to be used or collected in whole or in part for the purpose of serving as a factor in establishing the consumer's eligibility for

(A) credit or insurance to be used primarily for personal, family, or household purposes;

(B) employment purposes; or

(C) any other purpose authorized under section 604 [§ 1681b].

(2) *Exclusions.* Except as provided in paragraph (3), the term "consumer report" does not include

(A) subject to section 624, any

(i) report containing information solely as to transactions or experiences between the consumer and the person making the report;

(ii) communication of that information among persons related by common ownership or affiliated by corporate control; or

(iii) communication of other information among persons related by common ownership or affiliated by corporate control, if it is clearly and conspicuously disclosed to the consumer that the information may be communicated among such persons and the consumer is given the opportunity, before the time that the information is initially communicated, to direct that such information not be communicated among such persons;

(B) any authorization or approval of a specific extension of credit directly or indirectly by the issuer of a credit card or similar device;

(C) any report in which a person who has been requested by a third party to make a specific extension of credit directly or indirectly to a consumer conveys his or her decision with respect to such request, if the third party advises the consumer of the name and address of the person to whom the request was made, and such person makes the disclosures to the consumer required under section 615 [§ 1681m]; or

(D) a communication described in subsection (o) or (x).

(3) *Restriction on sharing of medical information.* Except for information or any communication of information disclosed as provided in sec-

tion 604(g)(3), the exclusions in paragraph (2) shall not apply with respect to information disclosed to any person related by common ownership or affiliated by corporate control, if the information is—

(A) medical information;

(B) an individualized list or description based on the payment transactions of the consumer for medical products or services; or

(C) an aggregate list of identified consumers based on payment transactions for medical products or services.

(e) The term "investigative consumer report" means a consumer report or portion thereof in which information on a consumer's character, general reputation, personal characteristics, or mode of living is obtained through personal interviews with neighbors, friends, or associates of the consumer reported on or with others with whom he is acquainted or who may have knowledge concerning any such items of information. However, such information shall not include specific factual information on a consumer's credit record obtained directly from a creditor of the consumer or from a consumer reporting agency when such information was obtained directly from a creditor of the consumer or from the consumer.

(f) The term "consumer reporting agency" means any person which, for monetary fees, dues, or on a cooperative nonprofit basis, regularly engages in whole or in part in the practice of assembling or evaluating consumer credit information or other information on consumers for the purpose of furnishing consumer reports to third parties, and which uses any means or facility of interstate commerce for the purpose of preparing or furnishing consumer reports.

(g) The term "file," when used in connection with information on any consumer, means all of the information on that consumer recorded and retained by a consumer reporting agency regardless of how the information is stored.

(h) The term "employment purposes" when used in connection with a consumer report means a report used for the purpose of evaluating a consumer for employment, promotion, reassignment or retention as an employee.

(i) The term "medical information"—

(1) means information or data, whether oral or recorded, in any form or medium, created by or derived from a health care provider or the consumer, that relates to—

(A) the past, present, or future physical, mental, or behavioral health or condition of an individual;

(B) the provision of health care to an individual; or

(C) the payment for the provision of health care to an individual.

(2) does not include the age or gender of a consumer, demographic

information about the consumer, including a consumer's residence address or e-mail address, or any other information about a consumer that does not relate to the physical, mental, or behavioral health or condition of a consumer, including the existence or value of any insurance policy.

(j) Definitions Relating to Child Support Obligations

(1) The "overdue support" has the meaning given to such term in section 666(e) of title 42 [Social Security Act, 42 U.S.C. § 666(e)].

(2) The term "State or local child support enforcement agency" means a State or local agency which administers a State or local program for establishing and enforcing child support obligations.

(k) Adverse Action

(1) *Actions included.* The term "adverse action"

(A) has the same meaning as in section 701(d)(6) of the Equal Credit Opportunity Act; and

(B) means

(i) a denial or cancellation of, an increase in any charge for, or a reduction or other adverse or unfavorable change in the terms of coverage or amount of, any insurance, existing or applied for, in connection with the underwriting of insurance;

(ii) a denial of employment or any other decision for employment purposes that adversely affects any current or prospective employee;

(iii) a denial or cancellation of, an increase in any charge for, or any other adverse or unfavorable change in the terms of, any license or benefit described in section 604(a)(3)(D) [§ 1681b]; and

(iv) an action taken or determination that is

(I) made in connection with an application that was made by, or a transaction that was initiated by, any consumer, or in connection with a review of an account under section 604(a)(3)(F)(ii)[§ 1681b]; and

(II) adverse to the interests of the consumer.

(2) *Applicable findings, decisions, commentary, and orders.* For purposes of any determination of whether an action is an adverse action under paragraph (1)(A), all appropriate final findings, decisions, commentary, and orders issued under section 701(d)(6) of the Equal Credit Opportunity Act by the Board of Governors of the Federal Reserve System or any court shall apply.

(1) The term "firm offer of credit or insurance" means any offer of credit or insurance to a consumer that will be honored if the consumer is determined, based on information in a consumer report on the consumer, to meet the specific criteria used to select the consumer for the offer, except that the offer may be further conditioned on one or more of the following:

(1) The consumer being determined, based on information in the consumer's application for the credit or insurance, to meet specific crite-

ria bearing on credit worthiness or insurability, as applicable, that are established

(A) before selection of the consumer for the offer; and

(B) for the purpose of determining whether to extend credit or insurance pursuant to the offer.

(2) Verification

(A) that the consumer continues to meet the specific criteria used to select the consumer for the offer, by using information in a consumer report on the consumer, information in the consumer's application for the credit or insurance, or other information bearing on the credit worthiness or insurability of the consumer; or

(B) of the information in the consumer's application for the credit or insurance, to determine that the consumer meets the specific criteria bearing on credit worthiness or insurability.

(3) The consumer furnishing any collateral that is a requirement for the extension of the credit or insurance that was

(A) established before selection of the consumer for the offer of credit or insurance; and

(B) disclosed to the consumer in the offer of credit or insurance.

(m) The term "credit or insurance transaction that is not initiated by the consumer" does not include the use of a consumer report by a person with which the consumer has an account or insurance policy, for purposes of

(1) reviewing the account or insurance policy; or

(2) collecting the account.

(n) The term "State" means any State, the Commonwealth of Puerto Rico, the District of Columbia, and any territory or possession of the United States.

(o) *Excluded communications.* A communication is described in this subsection if it is a communication

(1) that, but for subsection (d)(2)(D), would be an investigative consumer report;

(2) that is made to a prospective employer for the purpose of

(A) procuring an employee for the employer; or

(B) procuring an opportunity for a natural person to work for the employer;

(3) that is made by a person who regularly performs such procurement;

(4) that is not used by any person for any purpose other than a purpose described in subparagraph (A) or (B) of paragraph (2); and

(5) with respect to which

(A) the consumer who is the subject of the communication

(i) consents orally or in writing to the nature and scope of the communication, before the collection of any information for the purpose of making the communication;

(ii) consents orally or in writing to the making of the communication to a prospective employer, before the making of the communication; and

(iii) in the case of consent under clause (i) or (ii) given orally, is provided written confirmation of that consent by the person making the communication, not later than 3 business days after the receipt of the consent by that person;

(B) the person who makes the communication does not, for the purpose of making the communication, make any inquiry that if made by a prospective employer of the consumer who is the subject of the communication would violate any applicable Federal or State equal employment opportunity law or regulation; and

(C) the person who makes the communication

(i) discloses in writing to the consumer who is the subject of the communication, not later than 5 business days after receiving any request from the consumer for such disclosure, the nature and substance of all information in the consumer's file at the time of the request, except that the sources of any information that is acquired solely for use in making the communication and is actually used for no other purpose, need not be disclosed other than under appropriate discovery procedures in any court of competent jurisdiction in which an action is brought; and

(ii) notifies the consumer who is the subject of the communication, in writing, of the consumer's right to request the information described in clause (i).

(p) The term "consumer reporting agency that compiles and maintains files on consumers on a nationwide basis" means a consumer reporting agency that regularly engages in the practice of assembling or evaluating, and maintaining, for the purpose of furnishing consumer reports to third parties bearing on a consumer's credit worthiness, credit standing, or credit capacity, each of the following regarding consumers residing nationwide:

(1) Public record information.

(2) Credit account information from persons who furnish that information regularly and in the ordinary course of business.

(q) Definitions relating to fraud alerts.

(1) The term "active duty military consumer" means a consumer in military service who—

(A) is on active duty (as defined in section 101(d)(1) of title 10, United States Code) or is a reservist performing duty under a call or order to active duty under a provision of law referred to in section 101(a)(13) of title 10, United States Code; and

(B) is assigned to service away from the usual duty station of the consumer.

(2) The terms "fraud alert" and "active duty alert" mean a statement in the file of a consumer that—

(A) notifies all prospective users of a consumer report relating to the consumer that the consumer may be a victim of fraud, including identity theft, or is an active duty military consumer, as applicable; and

(B) is presented in a manner that facilitates a clear and conspicuous view of the statement described in subparagraph (A) by any person requesting such consumer report.

(3) The term "identity theft" means a fraud committed using the identifying information of another person, subject to such further definition as the Commission may prescribe, by regulation.

(4) The term "identity theft report" has the meaning given that term by rule of the Commission, and means, at a minimum, a report—

(A) that alleges an identity theft;

(B) that is a copy of an official, valid report filed by a consumer with an appropriate Federal, State, or local law enforcement agency, including the United States Postal Inspection Service, or such other government agency deemed appropriate by the Commission; and

(C) the filing of which subjects the person filing the report to criminal penalties relating to the filing of false information if, in fact, the information in the report is false.

(5) The term "new credit plan" means a new account under an open end credit plan (as defined in section 103(i) of the Truth in Lending Act) or a new credit transaction not under an open end credit plan.

(r) Credit and Debit Related Terms

(1) The term "card issuer" means—

(A) a credit card issuer, in the case of a credit card; and

(B) a debit card issuer, in the case of a debit card.

(2) The term "credit card" has the same meaning as in section 103 of the Truth in Lending Act.

(3) The term "debit card" means any card issued by a financial institution to a consumer for use in initiating an electronic fund transfer from the account of the consumer at such financial institution, for the purpose of transferring money between accounts or obtaining money, property, labor, or services.

(4) The terms "account" and "electronic fund transfer" have the same meanings as in section 903 of the Electronic Fund Transfer Act.

(5) The terms "credit" and "creditor" have the same meanings as in section 702 of the Equal Credit Opportunity Act.

(s) The term "Federal banking agency" has the same meaning as in section 3 of the Federal Deposit Insurance Act.

(t) The term "financial institution" means a State or National bank, a State or Federal savings and loan association, a mutual savings bank, a State or Federal credit union, or any other person that, directly or indirectly, holds a transaction account (as defined in section 19(b) of the Federal Reserve Act) belonging to a consumer.

(u) The term "reseller" means a consumer reporting agency that—

(1) assembles and merges information contained in the database of another consumer reporting agency or multiple consumer reporting agencies concerning any consumer for purposes of furnishing such information to any third party, to the extent of such activities; and

(2) does not maintain a database of the assembled or merged information from which new consumer reports are produced.

(v) The term "Commission" means the Federal Trade Commission.

(w) The term "nationwide specialty consumer reporting agency" means a consumer reporting agency that compiles and maintains files on consumers on a nationwide basis relating to—

(1) medical records or payments;

(2) residential or tenant history;

(3) check writing history;

(4) employment history; or

(5) insurance claims.

(x) Exclusion of Certain Communications for Employee Investigations

(1) A communication is described in this subsection if—

(A) but for subsection (d)(2)(D), the communication would be a consumer report;

(B) the communication is made to an employer in connection with an investigation of—

(i) suspected misconduct relating to employment; or

(ii) compliance with Federal, State, or local laws and regulations, the rules of a self-regulatory organization, or any preexisting written policies of the employer;

(C) the communication is not made for the purpose of investigating a consumer's credit worthiness, credit standing, or credit capacity; and

(D) the communication is not provided to any person except—

(i) to the employer or an agent of the employer;

(ii) to any Federal or State officer, agency, or department, or any officer, agency, or department of a unit of general local government;

(iii) to any self-regulatory organization with regulatory authority over the activities of the employer or employee;

(iv) as otherwise required by law; or

(v) pursuant to section 608.

(2) *Subsequent disclosure*. After taking any adverse action based in whole or in part on a communication described in paragraph (1), the employer shall disclose to the consumer a summary containing the nature and substance of the communication upon which the adverse action is based, except that the sources of information acquired solely for use in preparing what would be but for subsection (d)(2)(D) an investigative consumer report need not be disclosed.

(3) For purposes of this subsection, the term "self-regulatory organization" includes any self-regulatory organization (as defined in section 3(a)(26) of the Securities Exchange Act of 1934), any entity established under title I of the Sarbanes-Oxley Act of 2002, any board of trade designated by the Commodity Futures Trading Commission, and any futures association registered with such Commission.

§ 604. Permissible purposes of consumer reports [15 U.S.C. § 1681b]

(a) *In general*. Subject to subsection (c), any consumer reporting agency may furnish a consumer report under the following circumstances and no other:

(1) In response to the order of a court having jurisdiction to issue such an order, or a subpoena issued in connection with proceedings before a Federal grand jury.

(2) In accordance with the written instructions of the consumer to whom it relates.

(3) To a person which it has reason to believe

(A) intends to use the information in connection with a credit transaction involving the consumer on whom the information is to be furnished and involving the extension of credit to, or review or collection of an account of, the consumer; or

(B) intends to use the information for employment purposes; or

(C) intends to use the information in connection with the underwriting of insurance involving the consumer; or

(D) intends to use the information in connection with a determination of the consumer's eligibility for a license or other benefit granted by a governmental instrumentality required by law to consider an applicant's financial responsibility or status; or

(E) intends to use the information, as a potential investor or servicer, or current insurer, in connection with a valuation of, or an assessment of the credit or prepayment risks associated with, an existing credit obligation; or

(F) otherwise has a legitimate business need for the information

(i) in connection with a business transaction that is initiated by the consumer; or

(ii) to review an account to determine whether the consumer continues to meet the terms of the account.

(4) In response to a request by the head of a State or local child support enforcement agency (or a State or local government official authorized by the head of such an agency), if the person making the request certifies to the consumer reporting agency that

(A) the consumer report is needed for the purpose of establishing an individual's capacity to make child support payments or determining the appropriate level of such payments;

(B) the paternity of the consumer for the child to which the obligation relates has been established or acknowledged by the consumer in accordance with State laws under which the obligation arises (if required by those laws);

(C) the person has provided at least 10 days' prior notice to the consumer whose report is requested, by certified or registered mail to the last known address of the consumer, that the report will be requested; and

(D) the consumer report will be kept confidential, will be used solely for a purpose described in subparagraph (A), and will not be used in connection with any other civil, administrative, or criminal proceeding, or for any other purpose.

(5) To an agency administering a State plan under Section 454 of the Social Security Act (42 U.S.C. § 654) for use to set an initial or modified child support award.

(b) Conditions for Furnishing and Using Consumer Reports for Employment Purposes.

(1) *Certification from user.* A consumer reporting agency may furnish a consumer report for employment purposes only if

(A) the person who obtains such report from the agency certifies to the agency that

(i) the person has complied with paragraph (2) with respect to the consumer report, and the person will comply with paragraph (3) with respect to the consumer report if paragraph (3) becomes applicable; and

(ii) information from the consumer report will not be used in violation of any applicable Federal or State equal employment opportunity law or regulation; and

(B) the consumer reporting agency provides with the report, or has previously provided, a summary of the consumer's rights under this title, as prescribed by the Federal Trade Commission under section 609(c)(3) [§ 1681g].

(2) Disclosure to Consumer.

(A) *In general.* Except as provided in subparagraph (B), a person may not procure a consumer report, or cause a consumer report to be procured, for employment purposes with respect to any consumer, unless—

(i) a clear and conspicuous disclosure has been made in writing to the consumer at any time before the report is procured or caused to be procured, in a document that consists solely of the disclosure, that a consumer report may be obtained for employment purposes; and

(ii) the consumer has authorized in writing (which authorization may be made on the document referred to in clause (i)) the procurement of the report by that person.

(B) *Application by mail, telephone, computer, or other similar means.* If a consumer described in subparagraph (C) applies for employment by mail, telephone, computer, or other similar means, at any time before a consumer report is procured or caused to be procured in connection with that application—

(i) the person who procures the consumer report on the consumer for employment purposes shall provide to the consumer, by oral, written, or electronic means, notice that a consumer report may be obtained for employment purposes, and a summary of the consumer's rights under section 615(a)(3); and

(ii) the consumer shall have consented, orally, in writing, or electronically to the procurement of the report by that person.

(C) *Scope.* Subparagraph (B) shall apply to a person procuring a consumer report on a consumer in connection with the consumer's application for employment only if—

(i) the consumer is applying for a position over which the Secretary of Transportation has the power to establish qualifications and maximum hours of service pursuant to the provisions of section 31502 of title 49, or a position subject to safety regulation by a State transportation agency; and

(ii) as of the time at which the person procures the report or causes the report to be procured the only interaction between the consumer and the person in connection with that employment application has been by mail, telephone, computer, or other similar means.

(3) Conditions on use for adverse actions.

(A) *In general.* Except as provided in subparagraph (B), in using a consumer report for employment purposes, before taking any adverse action based in whole or in part on the report, the person intending to take such adverse action shall provide to the consumer to whom the report relates—

(i) a copy of the report; and

(ii) a description in writing of the rights of the consumer under this title, as prescribed by the Federal Trade Commission under section 609(c)(3).

(B) Application by mail, telephone, computer, or other similar means.

(i) If a consumer described in subparagraph (C) applies for employ-ment by mail, telephone, computer, or other similar means, and if a person who has procured a consumer report on the consumer for employment purposes takes adverse action on the employment application based in whole or in part on the report, then the person must provide to the consumer to whom the report relates, in lieu of the notices required under subparagraph (A) of this section and under section 615(a), within 3 business days of taking such action, an oral, written or electronic notification—

(I) that adverse action has been taken based in whole or in part on a consumer report received from a consumer reporting agency;

(II) of the name, address and telephone number of the consumer reporting agency that furnished the consumer report (including a toll-free telephone number established by the agency if the agency compiles and maintains files on consumers on a nationwide basis);

(III) that the consumer reporting agency did not make the decision to take the adverse action and is unable to provide to the consumer the specific reasons why the adverse action was taken; and

(IV) that the consumer may, upon providing proper identification, request a free copy of a report and may dispute with the consumer reporting agency the accuracy or completeness of any information in a report.

(ii) If, under clause (B)(i)(IV), the consumer requests a copy of a consumer report from the person who procured the report, then, within 3 business days of receiving the consumer's request, together with proper identification, the person must send or provide to the consumer a copy of a report and a copy of the consumer's rights as prescribed by the Federal Trade Commission under section 609(c)(3).

(C) *Scope.* Subparagraph (B) shall apply to a person procuring a consumer report on a consumer in connection with the consumer's application for employment only if—

(i) the consumer is applying for a position over which the Secretary of Transportation has the power to establish qualifications and maximum hours of service pursuant to the provisions of section 31502 of title 49, or a position subject to safety regulation by a State transportation agency; and

(ii) as of the time at which the person procures the report or causes the report to be procured the only interaction between the consumer and the person in connection with that employment application has been by mail, telephone, computer, or other similar means.

(4) Exception for national security investigations.

(A) *In general.* In the case of an agency or department of the United States Government which seeks to obtain and use a consumer report for employment purposes, paragraph (3) shall not apply to any adverse action by such agency or department which is based in part on such consumer report, if the head of such agency or department makes a written finding that—

(i) the consumer report is relevant to a national security investigation of such agency or department;

(ii) the investigation is within the jurisdiction of such agency or department;

(iii) there is reason to believe that compliance with paragraph (3) will—

(I) endanger the life or physical safety of any person;

(II) result in flight from prosecution;

(III) result in the destruction of, or tampering with, evidence relevant to the investigation;

(IV) result in the intimidation of a potential witness relevant to the investigation;

(V) result in the compromise of classified information; or

(VI) otherwise seriously jeopardize or unduly delay the investigation or another official proceeding.

(B) *Notification of consumer upon conclusion of investigation.* Upon the conclusion of a national security investigation described in subparagraph (A), or upon the determination that the exception under subparagraph (A) is no longer required for the reasons set forth in such subparagraph, the official exercising the authority in such subparagraph shall provide to the consumer who is the subject of the consumer report with regard to which such finding was made—

(i) a copy of such consumer report with any classified information redacted as necessary;

(ii) notice of any adverse action which is based, in part, on the consumer report; and

(iii) the identification with reasonable specificity of the nature of the investigation for which the consumer report was sought.

(C) *Delegation by head of agency or department.* For purposes of subparagraphs (A) and (B), the head of any agency or department of the United States Government may delegate his or her authorities under this paragraph to an official of such agency or department who has personnel security responsibilities and is a member of the Senior Executive Service or equivalent civilian or military rank.

(D) *Report to the Congress.* Not later than January 31 of each year, the head of each agency and department of the United States Government that exercised authority under this paragraph during the preceding year shall submit a report to the Congress on the number of times the department or agency exercised such authority during the year.

(E) *Definitions*. For purposes of this paragraph, the following definitions shall apply:

(i) The term "classified information" means information that is protected from unauthorized disclosure under Executive Order No. 12958 or successor orders.

(ii) The term "national security investigation" means any official inquiry by an agency or department of the United States Government to determine the eligibility of a consumer to receive access or continued access to classified information or to determine whether classified information has been lost or compromised.

(c) Furnishing reports in connection with credit or insurance transactions that are not initiated by the consumer.

(1) *In general*. A consumer reporting agency may furnish a consumer report relating to any consumer pursuant to subparagraph (A) or (C) of subsection (a)(3) in connection with any credit or insurance transaction that is not initiated by the consumer only if

(A) the consumer authorizes the agency to provide such report to such person; or

(B)(i) the transaction consists of a firm offer of credit or insurance;

(ii) the consumer reporting agency has complied with subsection (e); and

(iii) there is not in effect an election by the consumer, made in accordance with subsection (e), to have the consumer's name and address excluded from lists of names provided by the agency pursuant to this paragraph.

(2) *Limits on information received under paragraph (1)(B)*. A person may receive pursuant to paragraph (1)(B) only

(A) the name and address of a consumer;

(B) an identifier that is not unique to the consumer and that is used by the person solely for the purpose of verifying the identity of the consumer; and

(C) other information pertaining to a consumer that does not identify the relationship or experience of the consumer with respect to a particular creditor or other entity.

(3) *Information regarding inquiries*. Except as provided in   n 609(a)(5) [§ 1681g], a consumer reporting agency shall not any person a record of inquiries in connection with a credit transaction that is not initiated by a consumer.

(d) Reserved.

(e) Election of consumer to be excluded from lists.

(1) *In general*. A consumer may elect to have th

and address excluded from any list provided by a consumer reporting agency under subsection (c)(l)(B) in connection with a credit or insurance transaction that is not initiated by the consumer, by notifying the agency in accordance with paragraph (2) that the consumer does not consent to any use of a consumer report relating to the consumer in connection with any credit or insurance transaction that is not initiated by the consumer.

(2) *Manner of notification.* A consumer shall notify a consumer reporting agency under paragraph (1)

(A) through the notification system maintained by the agency under paragraph (5); or

(B) by submitting to the agency a signed notice of election form issued by the agency for purposes of this subparagraph.

(3) *Response of agency after notification through system.* Upon receipt of notification of the election of a consumer under paragraph (1) through the notification system maintained by the agency under paragraph (5), a consumer reporting agency shall

(A) inform the consumer that the election is effective only for the 5-year period following the election if the consumer does not submit to the agency a signed notice of election form issued by the agency for purposes of paragraph (2)(B); and

(B) provide to the consumer a notice of election form, if requested by the consumer, not later than 5 business days after receipt of the notification of the election through the system established under paragraph (5), in the case of a request made at the time the consumer provides notification through the system.

(4) *Effectiveness of election.* An election of a consumer under paragraph (1)

(A) shall be effective with respect to a consumer reporting agency beginning 5 business days after the date on which the consumer notifies the agency in accordance with paragraph (2);

(B) shall be effective with respect to a consumer reporting agency

(i) subject to subparagraph (C), during the 5-year period beginning 5 business days after the date on which the consumer notifies the agency of the election, in the case of an election for which a consumer notifies the agency only in accordance with paragraph (2)(A); or

(ii) until the consumer notifies the agency under subparagraph (C), in the case of an election for which a consumer notifies the agency in accordance with paragraph (2)(B);

(C) shall not be effective after the date on which the consumer notifies the agency, through the notification system established by the agency under paragraph (5), that the election is no longer effective; and

(D) shall be effective with respect to each affiliate of the agency.

(5) Notification System

(A) *In general.* Each consumer reporting agency that, under subsection (c)(l)(B), furnishes a consumer report in connection with a credit or insurance transaction that is not initiated by a consumer, shall

(i) establish and maintain a notification system, including a toll-free telephone number, which permits any consumer whose consumer report is maintained by the agency to notify the agency, with appropriate identification, of the consumer's election to have the consumer's name and address excluded from any such list of names and addresses provided by the agency for such a transaction; and

(ii) publish by not later than 365 days after the date of enactment of the Consumer Credit Reporting Reform Act of 1996, and not less than annually thereafter, in a publication of general circulation in the area served by the agency

(I) a notification that information in consumer files maintained by the agency may be used in connection with such transactions; and

(II) the address and toll-free telephone number for consumers to use to notify the agency of the consumer's election under clause (I).

(B) *Establishment and maintenance as compliance.* Establishment and maintenance of a notification system (including a toll-free telephone number) and publication by a consumer reporting agency on the agency's own behalf and on behalf of any of its affiliates in accordance with this paragraph is deemed to be compliance with this paragraph by each of those affiliates.

(6) *Notification system by agencies that operate nationwide.* Each consumer reporting agency that compiles and maintains files on consumers on a nationwide basis shall establish and maintain a notification system for purposes of paragraph (5) jointly with other such consumer reporting agencies.

(f) *Certain use or obtaining of information prohibited.* A person shall not use or obtain a consumer report for any purpose unless

(1) the consumer report is obtained for a purpose for which the consumer report is authorized to be furnished under this section; and

(2) the purpose is certified in accordance with section 607 [§ 1681e] by a prospective user of the report through a general or specific certification.

(g) Protection of Medical Information

(1) *Limitation on consumer reporting agencies.* A consumer reporting agency shall not furnish for employment purposes, or in connection with a credit or insurance transaction, a consumer report that contains medical information (other than medical contact information treated in the manner required under section 605(a)(6)) about a consumer, unless—

(A) if furnished in connection with an insurance transaction, the consumer affirmatively consents to the furnishing of the report;

(B) if furnished for employment purposes or in connection with a credit transaction—

(i) the information to be furnished is relevant to process or effect the employment or credit transaction; and

(ii) the consumer provides specific written consent for the furnishing of the report that describes in clear and conspicuous language the use for which the information will be furnished; or

(C) the information to be furnished pertains solely to transactions, accounts, or balances relating to debts arising from the receipt of medical services, products, or devises, where such information, other than account status or amounts, is restricted or reported using codes that do not identify, or do not provide information sufficient to infer, the specific provider or the nature of such services, products, or devices, as provided in section 605(a)(6).

(2) *Limitation on creditors.* Except as permitted pursuant to paragraph (3)(C) or regulations prescribed under paragraph (5)(A), a creditor shall not obtain or use medical information (other than medical contact information treated in the manner required under section 605(a)(6)) pertaining to a consumer in connection with any determination of the consumer's eligibility, or continued eligibility, for credit.

(3) *Actions authorized by federal law, insurance activities and regulatory determinations.* Section 603(d)(3) shall not be construed so as to treat information or any communication of information as a consumer report if the information or communication is disclosed—

(A) in connection with the business of insurance or annuities, including the activities described in section 18B of the model Privacy of Consumer Financial and Health Information Regulation issued by the National Association of Insurance Commissioners (as in effect on January 1, 2003);

(B) for any purpose permitted without authorization under the Standards for Individually Identifiable Health Information promulgated by the Department of Health and Human Services pursuant to the Health Insurance Portability and Accountability Act of 1996, or referred to under section 1179 of such Act, or described in section 502(e) of Public Law 106–102; or

(C) as otherwise determined to be necessary and appropriate, by regulation or order and subject to paragraph (6), by the Commission, any Federal banking agency or the National Credit Union Administration (with respect to any financial institution subject to the jurisdiction of such agency or Administration under paragraph (1), (2), or (3) of section 621(b), or the applicable State insurance authority (with respect to any person engaged in providing insurance or annuities).

(4) *Limitation on redisclosure of medical information.* Any person that

receives medical information pursuant to paragraph (1) or (3) shall not disclose such information to any other person, except as necessary to carry out the purpose for which the information was initially disclosed, or as otherwise permitted by statute, regulation, or order.

(5) Regulations and Effective Date for Paragraph (2)

(A) *Regulations required.* Each Federal banking agency and the National Credit Union Administration shall, subject to paragraph (6) and after notice and opportunity for comment, prescribe regulations that permit transactions under paragraph (2) that are determined to be necessary and appropriate to protect legitimate operational, transactional, risk, consumer, and other needs (and which shall include permitting actions necessary for administrative verification purposes), consistent with the intent of paragraph (2) to restrict the use of medical information for inappropriate purposes.

(B) *Final regulations required.* The Federal banking agencies and the National Credit Union Administration shall issue the regulations required under subparagraph (A) in final form before the end of the 6-month period beginning on the date of enactment of the Fair and Accurate Credit Transactions Act of 2003.

(6) *Coordination with other laws.* No provision of this subsection shall be construed as altering, affecting, or superseding the applicability of any other provision of Federal law relating to medical confidentiality.

§ 605. Requirements relating to information contained in consumer reports [15 U.S.C. §1681c]

(a) *Information excluded from consumer reports.* Except as authorized under subsection

(b) of this section, no consumer reporting agency may make any consumer report containing any of the following items of information:

(1) Cases under title 11 [United States Code] or under the Bankruptcy Act that, from the date of entry of the order for relief or the date of adjudication, as the case may be, antedate the report by more than 10 years.

(2) Civil suits, civil judgments, and records of arrest that from date of entry, antedate the report by more than seven years or until the governing statute of limitations has expired, whichever is the longer period.

(3) Paid tax liens which, from date of payment, antedate the report by more than seven years.

(4) Accounts placed for collection or charged to profit and loss which antedate the report by more than seven years.

(5) Any other adverse item of information, other than records of convictions of crimes which antedates the report by more than seven years.

(6) The name, address, and telephone number of any medical information furnisher that has notified the agency of its status, unless—

(A) such name, address, and telephone number are restricted or reported using codes that do not identify, or provide information sufficient to infer, the specific provider or the nature of such services, products, or devices to a person other than the consumer; or

(B) the report is being provided to an insurance company for a purpose relating to engaging in the business of insurance other than property and casualty insurance.

(b) *Exempted cases.* The provisions of paragraphs (1) through (5) of subsection (a) of this section are not applicable in the case of any consumer credit report to be used in connection with

(1) a credit transaction involving, or which may reasonably be expected to involve, a principal amount of $150,000 or more;

(2) the underwriting of life insurance involving, or which may reasonably be expected to involve, a face amount of $150,000 or more; or

(3) the employment of any individual at an annual salary which equals, or which may reasonably be expected to equal $75,000, or more.

(c) Running of Reporting Period

(1) *In general.* The 7-year period referred to in paragraphs (4) and (6)

(a) shall begin, with respect to any delinquent account that is placed for collection (internally or by referral to a third party, whichever is earlier), charged to profit and loss, or subjected to any similar action, upon the expiration of the 180-day period beginning on the date of the commencement of the delinquency which immediately preceded the collection activity, charge to profit and loss, or similar action.

(2) *Effective date.* Paragraph (1) shall apply only to items of information added to the file of a consumer on or after the date that is 455 days after the date of enactment of the Consumer Credit Reporting Reform Act of 1996.

(d) Information Required to be Disclosed

(1) *Title 11 information.* Any consumer reporting agency that furnishes a consumer report that contains information regarding any case involving the consumer that arises under title 11, United States Code, shall include in the report an identification of the chapter of such title 11 under which such case arises if provided by the source of the information. If any case arising or filed under title 11, United States Code, is withdrawn by the consumer before a final judgment, the consumer reporting agency shall include in the report that such case or filing was withdrawn upon receipt of documentation certifying such withdrawal.

(2) *Key factor in credit score information.* Any consumer reporting agency that furnishes a consumer report that contains any credit score or any other risk score or predictor on any consumer shall include in the report a clear and conspicuous statement that a key factor (as defined in section 609(f)(2)(B)) that adversely affected such score or predictor was

the number of enquiries, if such a predictor was in fact a key factor that adversely affected such score. This paragraph shall not apply to a check services company, acting as such, which issues authorizations for the purpose of approving or processing negotiable instruments, electronic fund transfers, or similar methods of payments, but only to the extent that such company is engaged in such activities.

(e) *Indication of closure of account by consumer.* If a consumer reporting agency is notified pursuant to section 623(a)(4) [§ 1681s-2] that a credit account of a consumer was voluntarily closed by the consumer, the agency shall indicate that fact in any consumer report that includes information related to the account.

(f) *Indication of dispute by consumer.* If a consumer reporting agency is notified pursuant to section 623(a)(3) [§ 1681s-2] that information regarding a consumer who was furnished to the agency is disputed by the consumer, the agency shall indicate that fact in each consumer report that includes the disputed information.

(g) Truncation of Credit Card and Debit Card Numbers

(1) *In general.* Except as otherwise provided in this subsection, no person that accepts credit cards or debit cards for the transaction of business shall print more than the last 5 digits of the card number or the expiration date upon any receipt provided to the cardholder at the point of the sale or transaction.

(2) *Limitation.* This subsection shall apply only to receipts that are electronically printed, and shall not apply to transactions in which the sole means of recording a credit card or debit card account number is by handwriting or by an imprint or copy of the card.

(3) *Effective date.* This subsection shall become effective—

(A) 3 years after the date of enactment of this subsection, with respect to any cash register or other machine or device that electronically prints receipts for credit card or debit card transactions that is in use before January 1, 2005; and

(B) 1 year after the date of enactment of this subsection, with respect to any cash register or other machine or device that electronically prints receipts for credit card or debit card transactions that is first put into use on or after January 1, 2005.

(h) Notice of Discrepancy in Address

(1) *In general.* If a person has requested a consumer report relating to a consumer from a consumer reporting agency described in section 603(p), the request includes an address for the consumer that substantially differs from the addresses in the file of the consumer, and the agency provides a consumer report in response to the request, the consumer reporting agency shall notify the requester of the existence of the discrepancy.

(2) Regulations

(A) *Regulations required.* The Federal banking agencies, the National Credit Union Administration, and the Commission shall jointly, with respect to the entities that are subject to their respective enforcement authority under section 621, prescribe regulations providing guidance regarding reasonable policies and procedures that a user of a consumer report should employ when such user has received a notice of discrepancy under paragraph (1).

(B) *Policies and procedures to be included.* The regulations prescribed under subparagraph (A) shall describe reasonable policies and procedures for use by a user of a consumer report—

(i) to form a reasonable belief that the user knows the identity of the person to whom the consumer report pertains; and

(ii) if the user establishes a continuing relationship with the consumer, and the user regularly and in the ordinary course of business furnishes information to the consumer reporting agency from which the notice of discrepancy pertaining to the consumer was obtained, to reconcile the address of the consumer with the consumer reporting agency by furnishing such address to such consumer reporting agency as part of information regularly furnished by the user for the period in which the relationship is established.

§ 605A. Identity theft prevention; fraud alerts and active duty alerts [15 U.S.C. §1681c-1]

(a) One-call Fraud Alerts

(1) *Initial alerts.* Upon the direct request of a consumer, or an individual acting on behalf of or as a personal representative of a consumer, who asserts in good faith a suspicion that the consumer has been or is about to become a victim of fraud or related crime, including identity theft, a consumer reporting agency described in section 603(p) that maintains a file on the consumer and has received appropriate proof of the identity of the requester shall—

(A) include a fraud alert in the file of that consumer, and also provide that alert along with any credit score generated in using that file, for a period of not less than 90 days, beginning on the date of such request, unless the consumer or such representative requests that such fraud alert be removed before the end of such period, and the agency has received appropriate proof of the identity of the requester for such purpose; and

(B) refer the information regarding the fraud alert under this paragraph to each of the other consumer reporting agencies described in section 603(p), in accordance with procedures developed under section 621(f).

(2) *Access to free reports.* In any case in which a consumer reporting agency includes a fraud alert in the file of a consumer pursuant to this subsection, the consumer reporting agency shall—

(A) disclose to the consumer that the consumer may request a free copy of the file of the consumer pursuant to section 612(d); and

(B) provide to the consumer all disclosures required to be made under section 609, without charge to the consumer, not later than 3 business days after any request described in subparagraph (A).

(b) Extended Alerts

(1) *In general.* Upon the direct request of a consumer, or an individual acting on behalf of or as a personal representative of a consumer, who submits an identity theft report to a consumer reporting agency described in section 603(p) that maintains a file on the consumer, if the agency has received appropriate proof of the identity of the requester, the agency shall—

(A) include a fraud alert in the file of that consumer, and also provide that alert along with any credit score generated in using that file, during the 7-year period beginning on the date of such request, unless the consumer or such representative requests that such fraud alert be removed before the end of such period and the agency has received appropriate proof of the identity of the requester for such purpose;

(B) during the 5-year period beginning on the date of such request, exclude the consumer from any list of consumers prepared by the consumer reporting agency and provided to any third party to offer credit or insurance to the consumer as part of a transaction that was not initiated by the consumer, unless the consumer or such representative requests that such exclusion be rescinded before the end of such period; and

(C) refer the information regarding the extended fraud alert under this paragraph to each of the other consumer reporting agencies described in section 603(p), in accordance with procedures developed under section 621(f).

(2) *Access to free reports.* In any case in which a consumer reporting agency includes a fraud alert in the file of a consumer pursuant to this subsection, the consumer reporting agency shall—

(A) disclose to the consumer that the consumer may request 2 free copies of the file of the consumer pursuant to section 612(d) during the 12-month period beginning on the date on which the fraud alert was included in the file; and

(B) provide to the consumer all disclosures required to be made under section 609, without charge to the consumer, not later than 3 business days after any request described in subparagraph (A).

(c) *Active duty alerts.* Upon the direct request of an active duty military consumer, or an individual acting on behalf of or as a personal representative of an active duty military consumer, a consumer reporting agency described in section 603(p) that maintains a file on the active duty military consumer and has received appropriate proof of the identity of the requester shall—

(1) include an active duty alert in the file of that active duty military consumer, and also provide that alert along with any credit score generated in using that file, during a period of not less than 12 months, or such longer period as the Commission shall determine, by regulation, beginning on the date of the request, unless the active duty military consumer or such representative requests that such fraud alert be removed before the end of such period, and the agency has received appropriate proof of the identity of the requester for such purpose;

(2) during the 2-year period beginning on the date of such request, exclude the active duty military consumer from any list of consumers prepared by the consumer reporting agency and provided to any third party to offer credit or insurance to the consumer as part of a transaction that was not initiated by the consumer, unless the consumer requests that such exclusion be rescinded before the end of such period; and

(3) refer the information regarding the active duty alert to each of the other consumer reporting agencies described in section 603(p), in accordance with procedures developed under section 621(f).

(d) *Procedures*. Each consumer reporting agency described in section 603(p) shall establish policies and procedures to comply with this section, including procedures that inform consumers of the availability of initial, extended, and active duty alerts and procedures that allow consumers and active duty military consumers to request initial, extended, or active duty alerts (as applicable) in a simple and easy manner, including by telephone.

(e) *Referrals of alerts*. Each consumer reporting agency described in section 603(p) that receives a referral of a fraud alert or active duty alert from another consumer reporting agency pursuant to this section shall, as though the agency received the request from the consumer directly, follow the procedures required under—

(1) paragraphs (1)(A) and (2) of subsection (a), in the case of a referral under subsection (a)(1)(B);

(2) paragraphs (1)(A), (1)(B), and (2) of subsection (b), in the case of a referral under subsection (b)(1)(C); and

(3) paragraphs (1) and (2) of subsection (c), in the case of a referral under subsection (c)(3).

(f) *Duty of reseller to reconvey alert*. A reseller shall include in its report any fraud alert or active duty alert placed in the file of a consumer pursuant to this section by another consumer reporting agency.

(g) *Duty of other consumer reporting agencies to provide contact information*. If a consumer contacts any consumer reporting agency that is not described in section 603(p) to communicate a suspicion that the consumer has been or is about to become a victim of fraud or related crime, including identity theft, the agency shall provide information to the consumer on how to contact the Commission and the consumer reporting agencies described in section 603(p) to obtain more detailed information and request alerts under this section.

(h) Limitations on Use of Information for Credit Extensions

(1) Requirements for initial and active duty alerts—

(A) *Notification.* Each initial fraud alert and active duty alert under this section shall include information that notifies all prospective users of a consumer report on the consumer to which the alert relates that the consumer does not authorize the establishment of any new credit plan or extension of credit, other than under an open-end credit plan (as defined in section 103(i)), in the name of the consumer, or issuance of an additional card on an existing credit account requested by a consumer, or any increase in credit limit on an existing credit account requested by a consumer, except in accordance with subparagraph (B).

(B) Limitation on Users

(i) *In general.* No prospective user of a consumer report that includes an initial fraud alert or an active duty alert in accordance with this section may establish a new credit plan or extension of credit, other than under an open-end credit plan (as defined in section 103(i)), in the name of the consumer, or issue an additional card on an existing credit account requested by a consumer, or grant any increase in credit limit on an existing credit account requested by a consumer, unless the user utilizes reasonable policies and procedures to form a reasonable belief that the user knows the identity of the person making the request.

(ii) *Verification.* If a consumer requesting the alert has specified a telephone number to be used for identity verification purposes, before authorizing any new credit plan or extension described in clause (i) in the name of such consumer, a user of such consumer report shall contact the consumer using that telephone number or take reasonable steps to verify the consumer's identity and confirm that the application for a new credit plan is not the result of identity theft.

(2) Requirements for Extended Alerts

(A) *Notification.* Each extended alert under this section shall include information that provides all prospective users of a consumer report relating to a consumer with—

(i) notification that the consumer does not authorize the establishment of any new credit plan or extension of credit described in clause (i), other than under an open-end credit plan (as defined in section 103(i)), in the name of the consumer, or issuance of an additional card on an existing credit account requested by a consumer, or any increase in credit limit on an existing credit account requested by a consumer, except in accordance with subparagraph (B); and

(ii) a telephone number or other reasonable contact method designated by the consumer.

(B) *Limitation on users*. No prospective user of a consumer report or of a credit score generated using the information in the file of a consumer that includes an extended fraud alert in accordance with this section may establish a new credit plan or extension of credit, other than under an open-end credit plan (as defined in section 103(i)), in the name of the consumer, or issue an additional card on an existing credit account requested by a consumer, or any increase in credit limit on an existing credit account requested by a consumer, unless the user contacts the consumer in person or using the contact method described in subparagraph (A)(ii) to confirm that the application for a new credit plan or increase in credit limit, or request for an additional card is not the result of identity theft.

§ 605B. Block of information resulting from identity theft [15 U.S.C. §1681c-2]

(a) *Block*. Except as otherwise provided in this section, a consumer reporting agency shall block the reporting of any information in the file of a consumer that the consumer identifies as information that resulted from an alleged identity theft, not later than 4 business days after the date of receipt by such agency of

(1) appropriate proof of the identity of the consumer;

(2) a copy of an identity theft report;

(3) the identification of such information by the consumer; and

(4) a statement by the consumer that the information is not information relating to any transaction by the consumer.

(b) *Notification*. A consumer reporting agency shall promptly notify the furnisher of information identified by the consumer under subsection (a)—

(1) that the information may be a result of identity theft;

(2) that an identity theft report has been filed;

(3) that a block has been requested under this section; and

(4) of the effective dates of the block.

(c) Authority to Decline or Rescind

(1) *In general*. A consumer reporting agency may decline to block, or may rescind any block, of information relating to a consumer under this section, if the consumer reporting agency reasonably determines that—

(A) the information was blocked in error or a block was requested by the consumer in error;

(B) the information was blocked, or a block was requested by the consumer, on the basis of a material misrepresentation of fact by the consumer relevant to the request to block; or

(C) the consumer obtained possession of goods, services, or money as a result of the blocked transaction or transactions.

(2) *Notification to consumer.* If a block of information is declined or rescinded under this subsection, the affected consumer shall be notified promptly, in the same manner as consumers are notified of the reinsertion of information under section 611(a)(5)(B).

(3) *Significance of block.* For purposes of this subsection, if a consumer reporting agency rescinds a block, the presence of information in the file of a consumer prior to the blocking of such information is not evidence of whether the consumer knew or should have known that the consumer obtained possession of any goods, services, or money as a result of the block.

(d) Exception for Resellers

(1) *No reseller file.* This section shall not apply to a consumer reporting agency, if the consumer reporting agency—

(A) is a reseller;

(B) is not, at the time of the request of the consumer under subsection (a), otherwise furnishing or reselling a consumer report concerning the information identified by the consumer; and

(C) informs the consumer, by any means, that the consumer may report the identity theft to the Commission to obtain consumer information regarding identity theft.

(2) *Reseller with file.* The sole obligation of the consumer reporting agency under this section, with regard to any request of a consumer under this section, shall be to block the consumer report maintained by the consumer reporting agency from any subsequent use, if—

(A) the consumer, in accordance with the provisions of subsection (a), identifies, to a consumer reporting agency, information in the file of the consumer that resulted from identity theft; and

(B) the consumer reporting agency is a reseller of the identified information.

(3) *Notice.* In carrying out its obligation under paragraph (2), the reseller shall promptly provide a notice to the consumer of the decision to block the file. Such notice shall contain the name, address, and telephone number of each consumer reporting agency from which the consumer information was obtained for resale.

(e) *Exception for verification companies.* The provisions of this section do not apply to a check services company, acting as such, which issues authorizations for the purpose of approving or processing negotiable instruments, electronic fund transfers, or similar methods of payments, except that, beginning 4 business days after receipt of information described in paragraphs (1) through (3) of subsection (a), a check services company shall not report to a national consumer reporting agency described in section 603(p), any information identified in the subject identity theft report as resulting from identity theft.

(f) *Access to blocked information by law enforcement agencies.* No provision of this section shall be construed as requiring a consumer reporting agency to prevent a Federal, State, or local law enforcement agency from accessing blocked information in a consumer file to which the agency could otherwise obtain access under this title.

[omitted Section 606. Disclosure of investigative consumer reports]

§ 607. Compliance procedures [15 U.S.C. § 1681e]

(a) *Identity and purposes of credit users.* Every consumer reporting agency shall maintain reasonable procedures designed to avoid violations of section 605 [§ 1681c] and to limit the furnishing of consumer reports to the purposes listed under section 604 [§ 1681b] of this title. These procedures shall require that prospective users of the information identify themselves, certify the purposes for which the information is sought, and certify that the information will be used for no other purpose. Every consumer reporting agency shall make a reasonable effort to verify the identity of a new prospective user and the uses certified by such prospective user prior to furnishing such user a consumer report. No consumer reporting agency may furnish a consumer report to any person if it has reasonable grounds for believing that the consumer report will not be used for a purpose listed in section 604 [§ 1681b] of this title.

(b) *Accuracy of report.* Whenever a consumer reporting agency prepares a consumer report it shall follow reasonable procedures to assure maximum possible accuracy of the information concerning the individual about whom the report relates.

(c) *Disclosure of consumer reports by users allowed.* A consumer reporting agency may not prohibit a user of a consumer report furnished by the agency on a consumer from disclosing the contents of the report to the consumer, if adverse action against the consumer has been taken by the user based in whole or in part on the report.

(d) Notice to Users and Furnishers of Information

(1) *Notice requirement.* A consumer reporting agency shall provide to any person

(A) who regularly and in the ordinary course of business furnishes information to the agency with respect to any consumer; or

(B) to whom a consumer report is provided by the agency; a notice of such person's responsibilities under this title.

(2) *Content of notice.* The Federal Trade Commission shall prescribe

the content of notices under paragraph (1), and a consumer reporting agency shall be in compliance with this subsection if it provides a notice under paragraph (1) that is substantially similar to the Federal Trade Commission prescription under this paragraph.

(e) Procurement of Consumer Report for Resale

(1) *Disclosure.* A person may not procure a consumer report for purposes of reselling the report (or any information in the report) unless the person discloses to the consumer reporting agency that originally furnishes the report

(A) the identity of the end-user of the report (or information); and

(B) each permissible purpose under section 604 [§ 1681b] for which the report is furnished to the end-user of the report (or information).

(2) *Responsibilities of procurers for resale.* A person who procures a consumer report for purposes of reselling the report (or any information in the report) shall

(A) establish and comply with reasonable procedures designed to ensure that the report (or information) is resold by the person only for a purpose for which the report may be furnished under section 604 [§ 1681b], including by requiring that each person to which the report (or information) is resold and that resells or provides the report (or information) to any other person

(i) identifies each end user of the resold report (or information);

(ii) certifies each purpose for which the report (or information) will be used; and

(iii) certifies that the report (or information) will be used for no other purpose; and

(B) before reselling the report, make reasonable efforts to verify the identifications and certifications made under subparagraph (A).

(3) *Resale of consumer report to a federal agency or department.* Notwithstanding paragraph (1) or (2), a person who procures a consumer report for purposes of reselling the report (or any information in the report) shall not disclose the identity of the end-user of the report under paragraph (1) or (2) if —

(A) the end user is an agency or department of the United States Government which procures the report from the person for purposes of determining the eligibility of the consumer concerned to receive access or continued access to classified information (as defined in section 604(b)(4)(E)(i)); and

(B) the agency or department certifies in writing to the person reselling the report that nondisclosure is necessary to protect classified information or the safety of persons employed by or contracting with, or undergoing investigation for work or contracting with the agency or department.

[omitted Section 608. Disclosures to governmental agencies]

§ 609. Disclosures to consumers [15 U.S.C. § 1681 g]

(a) *Information on file; sources; report recipients.* Every consumer reporting agency shall, upon request, and subject to 610(a)(1) [§ 1681h], clearly and accurately disclose to the consumer:

(1) All information in the consumer's file at the time of the request except that—

(A) if the consumer to whom the file relates requests that the first 5 digits of the social security number (or similar identification number) of the consumer not be included in the disclosure and the consumer reporting agency has received appropriate proof of the identity of the requester, the consumer reporting agency shall so truncate such number in such disclosure; and

(B) nothing in this paragraph shall be construed to require a consumer reporting agency to disclose to a consumer any information concerning credit scores or any other risk scores or predictors relating to the consumer.

(2) The sources of the information; except that the sources of information acquired solely for use in preparing an investigative consumer report and actually use for no other purpose need not be disclosed: Provided, That in the event an action is brought under this title, such sources shall be available to the plaintiff under appropriate discovery procedures in the court in which the action is brought.

(3)(A) Identification of each person (including each end-user identified under section 607(e)(1) [§ 1681e]) that procured a consumer report

(i) for employment purposes, during the 2-year period preceding the date on which the request is made; or

(ii) for any other purpose, during the 1-year period preceding the date on which the request is made.

(B) An identification of a person under subparagraph (A) shall include

(i) the name of the person or, if applicable, the trade name (written in full) under which such person conducts business; and

(ii) upon request of the consumer, the address and telephone number of the person.

(C) Subparagraph (A) does not apply if—

(i) the end user is an agency or department of the United States Government that procures the report from the person for purposes of determining the eligibility of the consumer to whom the report relates to receive access or continued access to classified information (as defined in section 604(b)(4)(E)(i)); and

(ii) the head of the agency or department makes a written finding as prescribed under section 604(b)(4)(A).

(4) The dates, original payees, and amounts of any checks upon which is based any adverse characterization of the consumer, included in the file at the time of the disclosure.

(5) A record of all inquiries received by the agency during the 1-year period preceding the request that identified the consumer in connection with a credit or insurance transaction that was not initiated by the consumer.

(6) If the consumer requests the credit file and not the credit score, a statement that the consumer may request and obtain a credit score.

(b) *Exempt information.* The requirements of subsection (a) of this section respecting the disclosure of sources of information and the recipients of consumer reports do not apply to information received or consumer reports furnished prior to the effective date of this title except to the extent that the matter involved is contained in the files of the consumer reporting agency on that date.

(c) Summary of Rights to Obtain and Dispute Information in Consumer Reports and to Obtain Credit

(1) Commission Summary of Rights Required

(A) *In general.* The Commission shall prepare a model summary of the rights of consumers under this title.

(B) *Content of summary.* The summary of rights prepared under subparagraph

(A) shall include a description of —

(i) the right of a consumer to obtain a copy of a consumer report under subsection (a) from each consumer reporting agency;

(ii) the frequency and circumstances under which a consumer is entitled to receive a consumer report without charge under section 612;

(iii) the right of a consumer to dispute information in the file of the consumer under section 611;

(iv) the right of a consumer to obtain a credit score from a consumer reporting agency, and a description of how to obtain a credit score;

(v) the method by which a consumer can contact, and obtain a consumer report from, a consumer reporting agency without charge, as provided in the regulations of the Commission prescribed under section 211(c) of the Fair and Accurate Credit Transactions Act of 2003; and

(vi) the method by which a consumer can contact, and obtain a consumer report from, a consumer reporting agency described in section 603(w), as provided in the regulations of the Commission prescribed under section 612(a)(1)(C).

(C) *Availability of summary of rights.* The Commission shall—

(i) actively publicize the availability of the summary of rights prepared under this paragraph;

(ii) conspicuously post on its Internet website the availability of such summary of rights; and

(iii) promptly make such summary of rights available to consumers, on request.

(2) *Summary of rights required to be included with agency disclosures.* A consumer reporting agency shall provide to a consumer, with each written disclosure by the agency to the consumer under this section—

(A) the summary of rights prepared by the Commission under paragraph (1);

(B) in the case of a consumer reporting agency described in section 603(p), a toll-free telephone number established by the agency, at which personnel are accessible to consumers during normal business hours;

(C) a list of all Federal agencies responsible for enforcing any provision of this title, and the address and any appropriate phone number of each such agency, in a form that will assist the consumer in selecting the appropriate agency;

(D) a statement that the consumer may have additional rights under State law, and that the consumer may wish to contact a State or local consumer protection agency or a State attorney general (or the equivalent thereof) to learn of those rights; and

(E) a statement that a consumer reporting agency is not required to remove accurate derogatory information from the file of a consumer, unless the information is outdated under section 605 or cannot be verified.

(d) Summary of Rights of Identity Theft Victims

(1) *In general.* The Commission, in consultation with the Federal banking agencies and the National Credit Union Administration, shall prepare a model summary of the rights of consumers under this title with respect to the procedures for remedying the effects of fraud or identity theft involving credit, an electronic fund transfer, or an account or transaction at or with a financial institution or other creditor.

(2) *Summary of rights and contact information.* Beginning 60 days after the date on which the model summary of rights is prescribed in final form by the Commission pursuant to paragraph (1), if any consumer contacts a consumer reporting agency and expresses a belief that the consumer is a victim of fraud or identity theft involving credit, an electronic fund transfer, or an account or transaction at or with a financial institution or other creditor, the consumer reporting agency shall, in addition to any other action that the agency may take, provide the consumer with a summary of rights that contains all of the information required by the Commission under paragraph (1), and information on how to contact the Commission to obtain more detailed information.

(e) Information Available to Victims

(1) *In general.* For the purpose of documenting fraudulent transactions resulting from identity theft, not later than 30 days after the date of receipt of a request from a victim in accordance with paragraph (3), and subject to verification of the identity of the victim and the claim of identity theft in accordance with paragraph (2), a business entity that has provided credit to, provided for consideration products, goods, or services to, accepted payment from, or otherwise entered into a commercial transaction for consideration with, a person who has allegedly made unauthorized use of the means of identification of the victim, shall provide a copy of application and business transaction records in the control of the business entity, whether maintained by the business entity or by another person on behalf of the business entity, evidencing any transaction alleged to be a result of identity theft to—

(A) the victim;

(B) any Federal, State, or local government law enforcement agency or officer specified by the victim in such a request; or

(C) any law enforcement agency investigating the identity theft and authorized by the victim to take receipt of records provided under this subsection.

(2) *Verification of identity and claim.* Before a business entity provides any information under paragraph (1), unless the business entity, at its discretion, otherwise has a high degree of confidence that it knows the identity of the victim making a request under paragraph (1), the victim shall provide to the business entity—

(A) as proof of positive identification of the victim, at the election of the business entity—

(i) the presentation of a government-issued identification card;

(ii) personally identifying information of the same type as was provided to the business entity by the unauthorized person; or

(iii) personally identifying information that the business entity typically requests from new applicants or for new transactions, at the time of the victim's request for information, including any documentation described in clauses (i) and (ii); and

(B) as proof of a claim of identity theft, at the election of the business entity—

(i) a copy of a police report evidencing the claim of the victim of identity theft; and

(ii) a properly completed—

(I) copy of a standardized affidavit of identity theft developed and made available by the Commission; or

(II) an affidavit of fact that is acceptable to the business entity for that purpose.

(3) *Procedures.* The request of a victim under paragraph (1) shall—

(A) be in writing;

(B) be mailed to an address specified by the business entity, if any; and

(C) if asked by the business entity, include relevant information about any transaction alleged to be a result of identity theft to facilitate compliance with this section including—

(i) if known by the victim (or if readily obtainable by the victim), the date of the application or transaction; and

(ii) if known by the victim (or if readily obtainable by the victim), any other identifying information such as an account or transaction number.

(4) *No charge to victim.* Information required to be provided under paragraph (1) shall be so provided without charge.

(5) *Authority to decline to provide information.* A business entity may decline to provide information under paragraph (1) if, in the exercise of good faith, the business entity determines that—

(A) this subsection does not require disclosure of the information;

(B) after reviewing the information provided pursuant to paragraph (2), the business entity does not have a high degree of confidence in knowing the true identity of the individual requesting the information;

(C) the request for the information is based on a misrepresentation of fact by the individual requesting the information relevant to the request for information; or

(D) the information requested is Internet navigational data or similar information about a person's visit to a website or online service.

(6) *Limitation on liability.* Except as provided in section 621, sections 616 and 617 do not apply to any violation of this subsection.

(7) *Limitation on civil liability.* No business entity may be held civilly liable under any provision of Federal, State, or other law for disclosure, made in good faith pursuant to this subsection.

(8) *No new recordkeeping obligation.* Nothing in this subsection creates an obligation on the part of a business entity to obtain, retain, or maintain information or records that are not otherwise required to be obtained, retained, or maintained in the ordinary course of its business or under other applicable law.

(9) *Rule of Construction*

(A) *In general.* No provision of subtitle A of title V of Public Law 106-102, prohibiting the disclosure of financial information by a business entity to third parties shall be used to deny disclosure of information to the victim under this subsection.

(B) *Limitation.* Except as provided in subparagraph (A), nothing in this subsection permits a business entity to disclose information, including information to law enforcement under subparagraphs (B) and

(C) of paragraph (1), that the business entity is otherwise prohibited from disclosing under any other applicable provision of Federal or State law.

(10) *Affirmative defense.* In any civil action brought to enforce this subsection, it is an affirmative defense (which the defendant must establish by a preponderance of the evidence) for a business entity to file an affidavit or answer stating that—

(A) the business entity has made a reasonably diligent search of its available business records; and

(B) the records requested under this subsection do not exist or are not reasonably available.

(11) *Definition of victim.* For purposes of this subsection, the term "victim" means a consumer whose means of identification or financial information has been used or transferred (or has been alleged to have been used or transferred) without the authority of that consumer, with the intent to commit, or to aid or abet, an identity theft or a similar crime.

(12) *Effective date.* This subsection shall become effective 180 days after the date of enactment of this subsection.

(13) *Effectiveness study.* Not later than 18 months after the date of enactment of this subsection, the Comptroller General of the United States shall submit a report to Congress assessing the effectiveness of this provision.

(f) Disclosure of Credit Scores

(1) *In general.* Upon the request of a consumer for a credit score, a consumer reporting agency shall supply to the consumer a statement indicating that the information and credit scoring model may be different than the credit score that may be used by the lender, and a notice which shall include—

(A) the current credit score of the consumer or the most recent credit score of the consumer that was previously calculated by the credit reporting agency for a purpose related to the extension of credit;

(B) the range of possible credit scores under the model used;

(C) all of the key factors that adversely affected the credit score of the consumer in the model used, the total number of which shall not exceed 4, subject to paragraph (9);

(D) the date on which the credit score was created; and

(E) the name of the person or entity that provided the credit score or credit file upon which the credit score was created.

(2) *Definitions.* For purposes of this subsection, the following definitions shall apply:

(A) The term "credit score"—

(i) means a numerical value or a categorization derived from a statistical tool or modeling system used by a person who makes or arranges a loan to predict the likelihood of certain credit behaviors, including default (and the numerical value or the categorization derived from such analysis may also be referred to as a "risk predictor" or "risk score"); and

(ii) does not include—

(I) any mortgage score or rating of an automated underwriting system that considers one or more factors in addition to credit information, including the loan to value ratio, the amount of down payment, or the financial assets of a consumer; or

(II) any other elements of the underwriting process or underwriting decision.

(B) The term "key factors" means all relevant elements or reasons adversely affecting the credit score for the particular individual, listed in the order of their importance based on their effect on the credit score.

(3) *Timeframe and manner of disclosure.* The information required by this subsection shall be provided in the same timeframe and manner as the information described in subsection (a).

(4) *Applicability to certain uses.* This subsection shall not be construed so as to compel a consumer reporting agency to develop or disclose a score if the agency does not—

(A) distribute scores that are used in connection with residential real property loans; or

(B) develop scores that assist credit providers in understanding the general credit behavior of a consumer and predicting the future credit behavior of the consumer.

(5) Applicability to credit scores developed by another person.

(A) *In general.* This subsection shall not be construed to require a consumer reporting agency that distributes credit scores developed by another person or entity to provide a further explanation of them, or to process a dispute arising pursuant to section 611, except that the consumer reporting agency shall provide the consumer with the name and address and website for contacting the person or entity who developed the score or developed the methodology of the score.

(B) *Exception.* This paragraph shall not apply to a consumer reporting agency that develops or modifies scores that are developed by another person or entity.

(6) *Maintenance of credit scores not required.* This subsection shall not be construed to require a consumer reporting agency to maintain credit scores in its files.

(7) *Compliance in certain cases.* In complying with this subsection, a consumer reporting agency shall—

(A) supply the consumer with a credit score that is derived from a credit scoring model that is widely distributed to users by that consumer reporting agency in connection with residential real property loans or with a credit score that assists the consumer in understanding the credit scoring assessment of the credit behavior of the consumer and predictions about the future credit behavior of the consumer; and

(B) a statement indicating that the information and credit scoring model may be different than that used by the lender.

(8) *Fair and reasonable fee.* A consumer reporting agency may charge a fair and reasonable fee, as determined by the Commission, for providing the information required under this subsection.

(9) *Use of enquiries as a key factor.* If a key factor that adversely affects the credit score of a consumer consists of the number of enquiries made with respect to a consumer report, that factor shall be included in the disclosure pursuant to paragraph (1)(C) without regard to the numerical limitation in such paragraph.

(g) Disclosure of Credit Scores by Certain Mortgage Lenders

(1) *In general.* Any person who makes or arranges loans and who uses a consumer credit score, as defined in subsection (f), in connection with an application initiated or sought by a consumer for a closed end loan or the establishment of an open end loan for a consumer purpose that is secured by 1 to 4 units of residential real property (hereafter in this subsection referred to as the "lender") shall provide the following to the consumer as soon as reasonably practicable:

(A) Information Required under Subsection (f)

(i) *In general.* A copy of the information identified in subsection (f) that was obtained from a consumer reporting agency or was developed and used by the user of the information.

(ii) *Notice under subparagraph (D).* In addition to the information provided to it by a third party that provided the credit score or scores, a lender is only required to provide the notice contained in subparagraph (D).

(B) Disclosures in Case of Automated Underwriting System

(i) *In general.* If a person that is subject to this subsection uses an automated underwriting system to underwrite a loan, that person may satisfy the obligation to provide a credit score by disclosing a credit score and associated key factors supplied by a consumer reporting agency.

(ii) *Numerical credit score.* However, if a numerical credit score is generated by an automated underwriting system used by an enterprise, and that score is disclosed to the person, the score shall be disclosed to the consumer consistent with subparagraph (C).

(iii) *Enterprise defined.* For purposes of this subparagraph, the term "enterprise" has the same meaning as in paragraph (6) of section 1303 of the Federal Housing Enterprises Financial Safety and Soundness Act of 1992.

(C) *Disclosures of credit scores not obtained from a consumer reporting agency.* A person that is subject to the provisions of this subsection and that uses a credit score, other than a credit score provided by a consumer reporting agency, may satisfy the obligation to provide a credit score by disclosing a credit score and associated key factors supplied by a consumer reporting agency.

(D) *Notice to home loan applicants.* A copy of the following notice, which shall include the name, address, and telephone number of each consumer reporting agency providing a credit score that was used:

"Notice To The Home Loan Applicant

"In connection with your application for a home loan, the lender must disclose to you the score that a consumer reporting agency distributed to users and the lender used in connection with your home loan, and the key factors affecting your credit scores.

"The credit score is a computer generated summary calculated at the time of the request and based on information that a consumer reporting agency or lender has on file. The scores are based on data about your credit history and payment patterns. Credit scores are important because they are used to assist the lender in determining whether you will obtain a loan. They may also be used to determine what interest rate you may be offered on the mortgage. Credit scores can change over time, depending on your conduct, how your credit history and payment patterns change, and how credit scoring technologies change.

"Because the score is based on information in your credit history, it is very important that you review the credit-related information that is being furnished to make sure it is accurate. Credit records may vary from one company to another.

"If you have questions about your credit score or the credit information that is furnished to you, contact the consumer reporting agency at the address and telephone number provided with this notice, or contact the lender, if the lender developed or generated the credit score. The consumer reporting agency plays no part in the decision to take any action on the loan application and is unable to provide you with specific reasons for the decision on a loan application.

"If you have questions concerning the terms of the loan, contact the lender."

(E) *Actions not required under this subsection.* This subsection shall not require any person to—

(i) explain the information provided pursuant to subsection (f);

(ii) disclose any information other than a credit score or key factors, as defined in subsection (f);

(iii) disclose any credit score or related information obtained by the user after a loan has closed;

(iv) provide more than 1 disclosure per loan transaction; or

(v) provide the disclosure required by this subsection when another person has made the disclosure to the consumer for that loan transaction.

(F) No Obligation for Content

(i) *In general.* The obligation of any person pursuant to this subsection shall be limited solely to providing a copy of the information that was received from the consumer reporting agency.

(ii) *Limit on liability.* No person has liability under this subsection for the content of that information or for the omission of any information within the report provided by the consumer reporting agency.

(G) *Person defined as excluding enterprise.* As used in this subsection, the term "person" does not include an enterprise (as defined in paragraph (6) of section 1303 of the Federal Housing Enterprises Financial Safety and Soundness Act of 1992).

(2) Prohibition on Disclosure Clauses Null and Void

(A) *In general.* Any provision in a contract that prohibits the disclosure of a credit score by a person who makes or arranges loans or a consumer reporting agency is void.

(B) *No liability for disclosure under this subsection.* A lender shall not have liability under any contractual provision for disclosure of a credit score pursuant to this subsection.

§ 610. Conditions and form of disclosure to consumers [15 U.S.C. § 1681h]

(a) In General

(1) *Proper identification.* A consumer reporting agency shall require, as a condition of making the disclosures required under section 609 [§ 1681g], that the consumer furnish proper identification.

(2) *Disclosure in writing.* Except as provided in subsection (b), the disclosures required to be made under section 609 [§ 1681g] shall be provided under that section in writing.

(b) Other Forms of Disclosure

(1) *In general.* If authorized by a consumer, a consumer reporting agency may make the disclosures required under 609 [§ 1681g]

(A) other than in writing; and

(B) in such form as may be

(i) specified by the consumer in accordance with paragraph (2); and

(ii) available from the agency.

(2) *Form.* A consumer may specify pursuant to paragraph (1) that disclosures under section 609 [§ 1681g] shall be made

(A) in person, upon the appearance of the consumer at the place of business of the consumer reporting agency where disclosures are regularly provided, during normal business hours, and on reasonable notice;

(B) by telephone, if the consumer has made a written request for disclosure by telephone;

(C) by electronic means, if available from the agency; or

(D) by any other reasonable means that is available from the agency.

(c) *Trained personnel.* Any consumer reporting agency shall provide trained personnel to explain to the consumer any information furnished to him pursuant to section 609 [§ 1681g] of this title.

(d) *Persons accompanying consumer.* The consumer shall be permitted to be accompanied by one other person of his choosing, who shall furnish reasonable identification. A consumer reporting agency may require the consumer to furnish a written statement granting permission to the consumer reporting agency to discuss the consumer's file in such person's presence.

(e) *Limitation of liability.* Except as provided in sections 616 and 617 [§§ 1681n and 1681o] of this title, no consumer may bring any action or proceeding in the nature of defamation, invasion of privacy, or negligence with respect to the reporting of information against any consumer reporting agency, any user of information, or any person who furnishes information to a consumer reporting agency, based on information disclosed pursuant to section 609, 610, or 615 [§§ 1681g, 1681h, or 1681m] of this title or based on information disclosed by a user of a consumer report to or for a consumer against whom the user has taken adverse action, based in whole or in part on the report, except as to false information furnished with malice or willful intent to injure such consumer.

§ 611. Procedure in case of disputed accuracy [15 U.S.C. § 1681i]

(a) Reinvestigations of Disputed Information

(1) Reinvestigation Required

(A) *In general.* Subject to subsection (f), if the completeness or accuracy of any item of information contained in a consumer's file at a consumer reporting agency is disputed by the consumer and the consumer notifies the agency directly, or indirectly through a reseller, of such dispute, the agency shall, free of charge, conduct a reasonable reinvestigation to determine whether the disputed information is inaccurate and record the current status of the disputed information, or delete the item from the file in accordance with paragraph (5), before the end of the 30-day period beginning on the date on which the agency receives the notice of the dispute from the consumer or reseller.

(B) *Extension of period to reinvestigate.* Except as provided in subparagraph (C), the 30-day period described in subparagraph (A) may be extended for not more than 15 additional days if the consumer reporting agency receives information from the consumer during that 30-day period that is relevant to the reinvestigation.

(C) *Limitations on extension of period to reinvestigate.* Subparagraph (B) shall not apply to any reinvestigation in which, during the 30-day period described in subparagraph (A), the information that is the subject of the reinvestigation is found to be inaccurate or incomplete or the consumer reporting agency determines that the information cannot be verified.

(2) Prompt Notice of Dispute to Furnisher of Information

(A) *In general*. Before the expiration of the 5-business-day period beginning on the date on which a consumer reporting agency receives notice of a dispute from any consumer or a reseller in accordance with paragraph (1), the agency shall provide notification of the dispute to any person who provided any item of information in dispute, at the address and in the manner established with the person. The notice shall include all relevant information regarding the dispute that the agency has received from the consumer or reseller.

(B) *Provision of other information*. The consumer reporting agency shall promptly provide to the person who provided the information in dispute all relevant information regarding the dispute that is received by the agency from the consumer or the reseller after the period referred to in subparagraph (A) and before the end of the period referred to in paragraph (1)(A).

(3) Determination That Dispute Is Frivolous or Irrelevant

(A) *In general*. Notwithstanding paragraph (1), a consumer reporting agency may terminate a reinvestigation of information disputed by a consumer under that paragraph if the agency reasonably determines that the dispute by the consumer is frivolous or irrelevant, including by reason of a failure by a consumer to provide sufficient information to investigate the disputed information.

(B) *Notice of determination*. Upon making any determination in accordance with subparagraph (A) that a dispute is frivolous or irrelevant, a consumer reporting agency shall notify the consumer of such determination not later than 5 business days after making such determination, by mail or, if authorized by the consumer for that purpose, by any other means available to the agency.

(C) *Contents of notice*. A notice under subparagraph (B) shall include (i) the reasons for the determination under subparagraph (A); and (ii) identification of any information required to investigate the disputed information, which may consist of a standardized form describing the general nature of such information.

(4) *Consideration of consumer information*. In conducting any reinvestigation under paragraph (1) with respect to disputed information in the file of any consumer, the consumer reporting agency shall review and consider all relevant information submitted by the consumer in the period described in paragraph (1)(A) with respect to such disputed information.

(5) Treatment of Inaccurate or Unverifiable Information

(A) *In general*. If, after any reinvestigation under paragraph (1) of any information disputed by a consumer, an item of the information is found to be inaccurate or incomplete or cannot be verified, the consumer reporting agency shall—

(i) promptly delete that item of information from the file of the consumer, or modify that item of information, as appropriate, based on the results of the reinvestigation; and

(ii) promptly notify the furnisher of that information that the information has been modified or deleted from the file of the consumer.

(B) Requirements Relating to Reinsertion of Previously Deleted Material

(i) *Certification of accuracy of information.* If any information is deleted from a consumer's file pursuant to subparagraph (A), the information may not be reinserted in the file by the consumer reporting agency unless the person who furnishes the information certifies that the information is complete and accurate.

(ii) *Notice to consumer.* If any information that has been deleted from a consumer's file pursuant to subparagraph (A) is reinserted in the file, the consumer reporting agency shall notify the consumer of the reinsertion in writing not later than 5 business days after the reinsertion or, if authorized by the consumer for that purpose, by any other means available to the agency.

(iii) *Additional information.* As part of, or in addition to, the notice under clause (ii), a consumer reporting agency shall provide to a consumer in writing not later than 5 business days after the date of the reinsertion

(I) a statement that the disputed information has been reinserted;

(II) the business name and address of any furnisher of information contacted and the telephone number of such furnisher, if reasonably available, or of any furnisher of information that contacted the consumer reporting agency, in connection with the reinsertion of such information; and

(III) a notice that the consumer has the right to add a statement to the consumer's file disputing the accuracy or completeness of the disputed information.

(C) *Procedures to prevent reappearance.* A consumer reporting agency shall maintain reasonable procedures designed to prevent the reappearance in a consumer's file, and in consumer reports on the consumer, of information that is deleted pursuant to this paragraph (other than information that is reinserted in accordance with subparagraph (B)(i)).

(D) *Automated reinvestigation system.* Any consumer reporting agency that compiles and maintains files on consumers on a nationwide basis shall implement an automated system through which furnishers of information to that consumer reporting agency may report the results of a reinvestigation that finds incomplete or inaccurate information in a consumer's file to other such consumer reporting agencies.

(6) Notice of Results of Reinvestigation

(A) *In general.* A consumer reporting agency shall provide written notice to a consumer of the results of a reinvestigation under this subsection not later than 5 business days after the completion of the reinvestigation, by mail or, if authorized by the consumer for that purpose, by other means available to the agency.

(B) *Contents.* As part of, or in addition to, the notice under subparagraph (A), a consumer reporting agency shall provide to a consumer in writing before the expiration of the 5-day period referred to in subparagraph (A)

(i) a statement that the reinvestigation is completed;

(ii) a consumer report that is based upon the consumer's file as that file is revised as a result of the reinvestigation;

(iii) a notice that, if requested by the consumer, a description of the procedure used to determine the accuracy and completeness of the information shall be provided to the consumer by the agency, including the business name and address of any furnisher of information contacted in connection with such information and the telephone number of such furnisher, if reasonably available;

(iv) a notice that the consumer has the right to add a statement to the consumer's file disputing the accuracy or completeness of the information; and

(v) a notice that the consumer has the right to request under subsection

(d) that the consumer reporting agency furnish notifications under that subsection.

(7) *Description of reinvestigation procedure.* A consumer reporting agency shall provide to a consumer a description referred to in paragraph (6)(B)(iii) by not later than 15 days after receiving a request from the consumer for that description.

(8) *Expedited dispute resolution.* If a dispute regarding an item of information in a consumer's file at a consumer reporting agency is resolved in accordance with paragraph (5)(A) by the deletion of the disputed information by not later than 3 business days after the date on which the agency receives notice of the dispute from the consumer in accordance with paragraph (1)(A), then the agency shall not be required to comply with paragraphs (2), (6), and (7) with respect to that dispute if the agency

(A) provides prompt notice of the deletion to the consumer by telephone;

(B) includes in that notice, or in a written notice that accompanies a confirmation and consumer report provided in accordance with subparagraph (C), a statement of the consumer's right to request under subsection (d) that the agency furnish notifications under that subsection; and

(C) provides written confirmation of the deletion and a copy of a consumer report on the consumer that is based on the consumer's file after the deletion, not later than 5 business days after making the deletion.

(b) *Statement of dispute*. If the reinvestigation does not resolve the dispute, the consumer may file a brief statement setting forth the nature of the dispute. The consumer reporting agency may limit such statements to not more than one hundred words if it provides the consumer with assistance in writing a clear summary of the dispute.

(c) *Notification of consumer dispute in subsequent consumer reports*. Whenever a statement of a dispute is filed, unless there is reasonable grounds to believe that it is frivolous or irrelevant, the consumer reporting agency shall, in any subsequent report containing the information in question, clearly note that it is disputed by the consumer and provide either the consumer's statement or a clear and accurate codification or summary thereof.

(d) *Notification of deletion of disputed information*. Following any deletion of information which is found to be inaccurate or whose accuracy can no longer be verified or any notation as to disputed information, the consumer reporting agency shall, at the request of the consumer, furnish notification that the item has been deleted or the statement, codification or summary pursuant to subsection (b) or (c) of this section to any person specifically designated by the consumer who has within two years prior thereto received a consumer report for employment purposes, or within six months prior thereto received a consumer report for any other purpose, which contained the deleted or disputed information.

(e) Treatment of Complaints and Report to Congress

(1) *In general*. The Commission shall—

(A) compile all complaints that it receives that a file of a consumer that is maintained by a consumer reporting agency described in section 603(p) contains incomplete or inaccurate information, with respect to which, the consumer appears to have disputed the completeness or accuracy with the consumer reporting agency or otherwise utilized the procedures provided by subsection (a); and

(B) transmit each such complaint to each consumer reporting agency involved.

(2) *Exclusion*. Complaints received or obtained by the Commission pursuant to its investigative authority under the Federal Trade Commission Act shall not be subject to paragraph (1).

(3) *Agency responsibilities*. Each consumer reporting agency described in section 603(p) that receives a complaint transmitted by the Commission pursuant to paragraph (1) shall—

(A) review each such complaint to determine whether all legal obligations imposed on the consumer reporting agency under this title (including any obligation imposed by an applicable court or administrative order) have been met with respect to the subject matter of the complaint;

(B) provide reports on a regular basis to the Commission regarding the determinations of and actions taken by the consumer reporting agency, if any, in connection with its review of such complaints; and

(C) maintain, for a reasonable time period, records regarding the disposition of each such complaint that is sufficient to demonstrate compliance with this subsection.

(4) *Rulemaking authority.* The Commission may prescribe regulations, as appropriate to implement this subsection.

(5) *Annual report.* The Commission shall submit to the Committee on Banking, Housing, and Urban Affairs of the Senate and the Committee on Financial Services of the House of Representatives an annual report regarding information gathered by the Commission under this subsection.

(f) Reinvestigation Requirement Applicable to Resellers

(1) *Exemption from general reinvestigation requirement.* Except as provided in paragraph (2), a reseller shall be exempt from the requirements of this section.

(2) *Action required upon receiving notice of a dispute.* If a reseller receives a notice from a consumer of a dispute concerning the completeness or accuracy of any item of information contained in a consumer report on such consumer produced by the reseller, the reseller shall, within 5 business days of receiving the notice, and free of charge—

(A) determine whether the item of information is incomplete or inaccurate as a result of an act or omission of the reseller; and

(B) if (i) the reseller determines that the item of information is incomplete or inaccurate as a result of an act or omission of the reseller, not later than 20 days after receiving the notice, correct the information in the consumer report or delete it; or

(ii) if the reseller determines that the item of information is not incomplete or inaccurate as a result of an act or omission of the reseller, convey the notice of the dispute, together with all relevant information provided by the consumer, to each consumer reporting agency that provided the reseller with the information that is the subject of the dispute, using an address or a notification mechanism specified by the consumer reporting agency for such notices.

(3) *Responsibility of consumer reporting agency to notify consumer through reseller.* Upon the completion of a reinvestigation under this section of a dispute concerning the completeness or accuracy of any information in the file of a consumer by a consumer reporting agency that received notice of the dispute from a reseller under paragraph (2)—

(A) the notice by the consumer reporting agency under paragraph

(6), (7), or (8) of subsection (a) shall be provided to the reseller in lieu of the consumer; and

(B) the reseller shall immediately reconvey such notice to the consumer, including any notice of a deletion by telephone in the manner required under paragraph (8)(A).

(4) *Reseller reinvestigations.* No provision of this subsection shall be construed as prohibiting a reseller from conducting a reinvestigation of a consumer dispute directly.

§ 612. Charges for certain disclosures [15 U.S.C. § 1681j]

(a) Free Annual Disclosure

(1) Nationwide Consumer Reporting Agencies

(A) *In general.* All consumer reporting agencies described in subsections (p) and (w) of section 603 shall make all disclosures pursuant to section 609 once during any 12-month period upon request of the consumer and without charge to the consumer.

(B) *Centralized source.* Subparagraph (A) shall apply with respect to a consumer reporting agency described in section 603(p) only if the request from the consumer is made using the centralized source established for such purpose in accordance with section 211(c) of the Fair and Accurate Credit Transactions Act of 2003.

(C) Nationwide Specialty Consumer Reporting Agency

(i) *In general.* The Commission shall prescribe regulations applicable to each consumer reporting agency described in section 603(w) to require the establishment of a streamlined process for consumers to request consumer reports under subparagraph (A), which shall include, at a minimum, the establishment by each such agency of a toll-free telephone number for such requests.

(ii) *Considerations.* In prescribing regulations under clause (i), the Commission shall consider—

(I) the significant demands that may be placed on consumer reporting agencies in providing such consumer reports;

(II) appropriate means to ensure that consumer reporting agencies can satisfactorily meet those demands, including the efficacy of a system of staggering the availability to consumers of such consumer reports; and

(III) the ease by which consumers should be able to contact consumer reporting agencies with respect to access to such consumer reports.

(iii) *Date of issuance.* The Commission shall issue the regulations required by this subparagraph in final form not later than 6 months after the date of enactment of the Fair and Accurate Credit Transactions Act of 2003.

(iv) *Consideration of ability to comply.* The regulations of the Commission under this subparagraph shall establish an effective date by which each nationwide specialty consumer reporting agency (as defined in section 603(w)) shall be required to comply with subsection (a), which effective date—

(I) shall be established after consideration of the ability of each nationwide specialty consumer reporting agency to comply with subsection (a); and

(II) shall be not later than 6 months after the date on which such regulations are issued in final form (or such additional period not to exceed 3 months, as the Commission determines appropriate).

(2) *Timing.* A consumer reporting agency shall provide a consumer report under paragraph (1) not later than 15 days after the date on which the request is received under paragraph (1).

(3) *Reinvestigations.* Notwithstanding the time periods specified in section 611(a)(1), a reinvestigation under that section by a consumer reporting agency upon a request of a consumer that is made after receiving a consumer report under this subsection shall be completed not later than 45 days after the date on which the request is received.

(4) *Exception for first 12 months of operation.* This subsection shall not apply to a consumer reporting agency that has not been furnishing consumer reports to third parties on a continuing basis during the 12-month period preceding a request under paragraph (1), with respect to consumers residing nationwide.

(b) *Free disclosure after adverse notice to consumer.* Each consumer reporting agency that maintains a file on a consumer shall make all disclosures pursuant to section 609 [§ 1681g] without charge to the consumer if, not later than 60 days after receipt by such consumer of a notification pursuant to section 615 [§ 1681m], or of a notification from a debt collection agency affiliated with that consumer reporting agency stating that the consumer's credit rating may be or has been adversely affected, the consumer makes a request under section 609 [§ 1681g].

(c) *Free disclosure under certain other circumstances.* Upon the request of the consumer, a consumer reporting agency shall make all disclosures pursuant to section 609 [§ 1681g] once during any 12-month period without charge to that consumer if the consumer certifies in writing that the consumer

(1) is unemployed and intends to apply for employment in the 60-day period beginning on the date on which the certification is made;

(2) is a recipient of public welfare assistance; or

(3) has reason to believe that the file on the consumer at the agency contains inaccurate information due to fraud.

(d) *Free disclosures in connection with fraud alerts.* Upon the request of a consumer, a consumer reporting agency described in section 603(p) shall make all disclosures pursuant to section 609 without charge to the consumer, as provided in subsections (a)(2) and (b)(2) of section 605A, as applicable.

(e) *Other charges prohibited.* A consumer reporting agency shall not impose any charge on a consumer for providing any notification required by this title or making any disclosure required by this title, except as authorized by subsection (f).

(f) Reasonable Charges Allowed for Certain Disclosures

(1) *In general.* In the case of a request from a consumer other than a request that is covered by any of subsections (a) through (d), a consumer reporting agency may impose a reasonable charge on a consumer

(A) for making a disclosure to the consumer pursuant to section 609 [§ 1681g], which charge

(i) shall not exceed $8; and

(ii) shall be indicated to the consumer before making the disclosure; and

(B) for furnishing, pursuant to 611(d) [§ 1681i], following a reinvestigation under section 611(a) [§ 1681i], a statement, codification, or summary to a person designated by the consumer under that section after the 30-day period beginning on the date of notification of the consumer under paragraph (6) or (8) of section 611(a) [§ 1681i] with respect to the reinvestigation, which charge

(i) shall not exceed the charge that the agency would impose on each designated recipient for a consumer report; and

(ii) shall be indicated to the consumer before furnishing such information.

(2) *Modification of amount.* The Federal Trade Commission shall increase the amount referred to in paragraph (1)(A)(i) on January 1 of each year, based proportionally on changes in the Consumer Price Index, with fractional changes rounded to the nearest fifty cents.

§ 613. Public record information for employment purposes [15 U.S.C. § 1681k]

(a) *In general.* A consumer reporting agency which furnishes a consumer report for employment purposes and which for that purpose compiles and reports items of information on consumers which are matters of public record and are likely to have an adverse effect upon a consumer's ability to obtain employment shall

(1) at the time such public record information is reported to the user of such consumer report, notify the consumer of the fact that public record information is being reported by the consumer reporting agency, together with the name and address of the person to whom such information is being reported; or

(2) maintain strict procedures designed to insure that whenever public record information which is likely to have an adverse effect on a consumer's ability to obtain employment is reported it is complete and up to date. For purposes of this paragraph, items of public record relating to arrests, indictments, convictions, suits, tax liens, and outstanding judgments shall be considered up to date if the current public record status of the item at the time of the report is reported.

(b) *Exemption for national security investigations.* Subsection (a) does not apply in the case of an agency or department of the United States Government that seeks to obtain and use a consumer report for employment purposes, if the head of the agency or department makes a written finding as prescribed under section 604(b)(4)(A).

§ 614. Restrictions on investigative consumer reports [15 U.S.C. § 1681*l*]

Whenever a consumer reporting agency prepares an investigative consumer report, no adverse information in the consumer report (other than information which is a matter of public record) may be included in a subsequent consumer report unless such adverse information has been verified in the process of making such subsequent consumer report, or the adverse information was received within the three-month period preceding the date the subsequent report is furnished.

§ 615. Requirements on users of consumer reports [15 U.S.C. § 1681m]

(a) *Duties of users taking adverse actions on the basis of information contained in consumer reports.* If any person takes any adverse action with respect to any consumer that is based in whole or in part on any information contained in a consumer report, the person shall

(1) provide oral, written, or electronic notice of the adverse action to the consumer;

(2) provide to the consumer orally, in writing, or electronically

(A) the name, address, and telephone number of the consumer reporting agency (including a toll-free telephone number established by the agency if the agency compiles and maintains files on consumers on a nationwide basis) that furnished the report to the person; and

(B) a statement that the consumer reporting agency did not make the decision to take the adverse action and is unable to provide the consumer the specific reasons why the adverse action was taken; and

(3) provide to the consumer an oral, written, or electronic notice of the consumer's right

(A) to obtain, under section 612 [§ 1681j], a free copy of a consumer report on the consumer from the consumer reporting agency referred to in paragraph (2), which notice shall include an indication of the 60-day period under that section for obtaining such a copy; and

(B) to dispute, under section 611 [§ 1681i], with a consumer reporting agency the accuracy or completeness of any information in a consumer report furnished by the agency.

(b) Adverse Action Based on Information Obtained from Third Parties Other than Consumer Reporting Agencies

(1) *In general.* Whenever credit for personal, family, or household purposes involving a consumer is denied or the charge for such credit is increased either wholly or partly because of information obtained from a person other than a consumer reporting agency bearing upon the consumer's credit worthiness, credit standing, credit capacity, character, general reputation, personal characteristics, or mode of living, the user of such information shall, within a reasonable period of time, upon the consumer's written request for the reasons for such adverse action received within sixty days after learning of such adverse action, disclose the nature of the information to the consumer. The user of such information shall clearly and accurately disclose to the consumer his right to make such written request at the time such adverse action is communicated to the consumer.

(2) Duties of Person Taking Certain Actions Based on Information Provided by Affiliate

(A) *Duties, generally.* If a person takes an action described in subparagraph (B) with respect to a consumer, based in whole or in part on information described in subparagraph (C), the person shall

(i) notify the consumer of the action, including a statement that the consumer may obtain the information in accordance with clause (ii); and

(ii) upon a written request from the consumer received within 60 days after transmittal of the notice required by clause (i), disclose to the consumer the nature of the information upon which the action is based by not later than 30 days after receipt of the request.

(B) *Action described.* An action referred to in subparagraph (A) is an adverse action described in section 603(k)(1)(A) [§ 1681a], taken in connection with a transaction initiated by the consumer, or any adverse action described in clause (i) or (ii) of section 603(k)(1)(B) [§ 1681a].

(C) *Information described.* Information referred to in subparagraph (A)

(i) except as provided in clause (ii), is information that

(I) is furnished to the person taking the action by a person related by common ownership or affiliated by common corporate control to the person taking the action; and

(II) bears on the credit worthiness, credit standing, credit capacity, character, general reputation, personal characteristics, or mode of living of the consumer; and

(ii) does not include

(I) information solely as to transactions or experiences between the consumer and the person furnishing the information; or

(II) information in a consumer report.

(c) *Reasonable procedures to assure compliance.* No person shall be held liable for any violation of this section if he shows by a preponderance of the evidence that at the time of the alleged violation he maintained reasonable procedures to assure compliance with the provisions of this section.

(d) Duties of Users Making Written Credit or Insurance Solicitations on the Basis of Information Contained in Consumer Files

(1) *In general.* Any person who uses a consumer report on any consumer in connection with any credit or insurance transaction that is not initiated by the consumer, that is provided to that person under section 604(c)(1)(B) [§ 1681b], shall provide with each written solicitation made to the consumer regarding the transaction a clear and conspicuous statement that

(A) information contained in the consumer's consumer report was used in connection with the transaction;

(B) the consumer received the offer of credit or insurance because the consumer satisfied the criteria for credit worthiness or insurability under which the consumer was selected for the offer;

(C) if applicable, the credit or insurance may not be extended if, after the consumer responds to the offer, the consumer does not meet the criteria used to select the consumer for the offer or any applicable criteria bearing on credit worthiness or insurability or does not furnish any required collateral;

(D) the consumer has a right to prohibit information contained in the consumer's file with any consumer reporting agency from being used in connection with any credit or insurance transaction that is not initiated by the consumer; and

(E) the consumer may exercise the right referred to in subparagraph (D) by notifying a notification system established under section 604(e) [§ 1681b].

(2) *Disclosure of address and telephone number; format.* A statement under paragraph (1) shall—

(A) include the address and toll-free telephone number of the appropriate notification system established under section 604(e); and

(B) be presented in such format and in such type size and manner as to be simple and easy to understand, as established by the Commission, by rule, in consultation with the Federal banking agencies and the National Credit Union Administration.

(3) *Maintaining criteria on file.* A person who makes an offer of credit or insurance to a consumer under a credit or insurance transaction described in paragraph (1) shall maintain on file the criteria used to select the consumer to receive the offer, all criteria bearing on credit worthiness or insurability, as applicable, that are the basis for determining whether or not to extend credit or insurance pursuant to the offer, and any requirement for the furnishing of collateral as a condition of the extension of credit or insurance, until the expiration of the 3-year period beginning on the date on which the offer is made to the consumer.

(4) *Authority of federal agencies regarding unfair or deceptive acts or practices not affected.* This section is not intended to affect the authority of any Federal or State agency to enforce a prohibition against unfair or deceptive acts or practices, including the making of false or misleading statements in connection with a credit or insurance transaction that is not initiated by the consumer.

(e) Red Flag Guidelines and Regulations Required

(1) *Guidelines.* The Federal banking agencies, the National Credit Union Administration, and the Commission shall jointly, with respect to the entities that are subject to their respective enforcement authority under section 621—

(A) establish and maintain guidelines for use by each financial institution and each creditor regarding identity theft with respect to account holders at, or customers of, such entities, and update such guidelines as often as necessary;

(B) prescribe regulations requiring each financial institution and each creditor to establish reasonable policies and procedures for implementing the guidelines established pursuant to subparagraph (A), to identify possible risks to account holders or customers or to the safety and soundness of the institution or customers; and

(C) prescribe regulations applicable to card issuers to ensure that, if a card issuer receives notification of a change of address for an existing account, and within a short period of time (during at least the first 30 days after such notification is received) receives a request for an additional or replacement card for the same account, the card issuer may not issue the additional or replacement card, unless the card issuer, in accordance with reasonable policies and procedures—

(i) notifies the cardholder of the request at the former address of the cardholder and provides to the cardholder a means of promptly reporting incorrect address changes;

(ii) notifies the cardholder of the request by such other means of communication as the cardholder and the card issuer previously agreed to; or

(iii) uses other means of assessing the validity of the change of address, in accordance with reasonable policies and procedures established by the card issuer in accordance with the regulations prescribed under subparagraph (B).

(2) Criteria

(A) *In general.* In developing the guidelines required by paragraph (1)(A), the agencies described in paragraph (1) shall identify patterns, practices, and specific forms of activity that indicate the possible existence of identity theft.

(B) *Inactive accounts.* In developing the guidelines required by paragraph (1)(A), the agencies described in paragraph (1) shall consider including reasonable guidelines providing that when a transaction occurs with respect to a credit or deposit account that has been inactive for more than 2 years, the creditor or financial institution shall follow reasonable policies and procedures that provide for notice to be given to a consumer in a manner reasonably designed to reduce the likelihood of identity theft with respect to such account.

(3) *Consistency with verification requirements.* Guidelines established pursuant to paragraph (1) shall not be inconsistent with the policies and procedures required under section 5318(l) of title 31, United States Code.

(f) Prohibition on Sale or Transfer of Debt Caused by Identity Theft

(1) *In general.* No person shall sell, transfer for consideration, or place for collection a debt that such person has been notified under section 605B has resulted from identity theft.

(2) *Applicability.* The prohibitions of this subsection shall apply to all persons collecting a debt described in paragraph (1) after the date of a notification under paragraph (1).

(3) *Rule of construction.* Nothing in this subsection shall be construed to prohibit—

(A) the repurchase of a debt in any case in which the assignee of the debt requires such repurchase because the debt has resulted from identity theft;

(B) the securitization of a debt or the pledging of a portfolio of debt as collateral in connection with a borrowing; or

(C) the transfer of debt as a result of a merger, acquisition, purchase and assumption transaction, or transfer of substantially all of the assets of an entity.

(g) *Debt collector communications concerning identity theft.* If a person acting as a debt collector (as that term is defined in title VIII) on behalf of a third party that is a creditor or other user of a consumer report is notified that any information relating to a debt that the person is attempting to collect may be fraudulent or may be the result of identity theft, that person shall—

(1) notify the third party that the information may be fraudulent or may be the result of identity theft; and

(2) upon request of the consumer to whom the debt purportedly relates, provide to the consumer all information to which the consumer would otherwise be entitled if the consumer were not a victim of identity theft, but wished to dispute the debt under provisions of law applicable to that person.

(h) Duties of Users in Certain Credit Transactions

(1) *In general.* Subject to rules prescribed as provided in paragraph (6), if any person uses a consumer report in connection with an application for, or a grant, extension, or other provision of, credit on material terms that are materially less favorable than the most favorable terms available to a substantial proportion of consumers from or through that person, based in whole or in part on a consumer report, the person shall provide an oral, written, or electronic notice to the consumer in the form and manner required by regulations prescribed in accordance with this subsection.

(2) *Timing.* The notice required under paragraph (1) may be provided at the time of an application for, or a grant, extension, or other provision of, credit or the time of communication of an approval of an application for, or grant, extension, or other provision of, credit, except as provided in the regulations prescribed under paragraph (6).

(3) *Exceptions.* No notice shall be required from a person under this subsection if —

(A) the consumer applied for specific material terms and was granted those terms, unless those terms were initially specified by the person after the transaction was initiated by the consumer and after the person obtained a consumer report; or

(B) the person has provided or will provide a notice to the consumer under subsection (a) in connection with the transaction.

(4) *Other notice not sufficient.* A person that is required to provide a notice under subsection (a) cannot meet that requirement by providing a notice under this subsection.

(5) *Content and delivery of notice.* A notice under this subsection shall, at a minimum —

(A) include a statement informing the consumer that the terms offered to the consumer are set based on information from a consumer report;

(B) identify the consumer reporting agency furnishing the report;

(C) include a statement informing the consumer that the consumer may obtain a copy of a consumer report from that consumer reporting agency without charge; and

(D) include the contact information specified by that consumer reporting agency for obtaining such consumer reports (including a toll-free telephone number established by the agency in the case of a consumer reporting agency described in section 603(p)).

(6) Rulemaking

(A) *Rules required*. The Commission and the Board shall jointly prescribe rules.

(B) *Content*. Rules required by subparagraph (A) shall address, but are not limited to—

(i) the form, content, time, and manner of delivery of any notice under this subsection;

(ii) clarification of the meaning of terms used in this subsection, including what credit terms are material, and when credit terms are materially less favorable;

(iii) exceptions to the notice requirement under this subsection for classes of persons or transactions regarding which the agencies determine that notice would not significantly benefit consumers;

(iv) a model notice that may be used to comply with this subsection; and

(v) the timing of the notice required under paragraph (1), including the circumstances under which the notice must be provided after the terms offered to the consumer were set based on information from a consumer report.

(7) *Compliance*. A person shall not be liable for failure to perform the duties required by this section if, at the time of the failure, the person maintained reasonable policies and procedures to comply with this section.

(8) Enforcement

(A) *No civil actions*. Sections 616 and 617 shall not apply to any failure by any person to comply with this section.

(B) *Administrative enforcement*. This section shall be enforced exclusively under section 621 by the Federal agencies and officials identified in that section.

[omitted Section 616: Civil liability for willful noncompliance]

[omitted Section 617. Civil liability for negligent noncompliance]

[omitted Section 618. Jurisdiction of courts; limitation of actions]

[omitted Section 619. Obtaining information under false pretenses]

[omitted Section 620. Unauthorized disclosures by officers or employees]

[omitted Section 621. Administrative enforcement]

[omitted Section 622. Information on overdue child support obligations]

§ 623. Responsibilities of furnishers of information to consumer reporting agencies [15 U.S.C. § 1681s-2]

(a) Duty of Furnishers of Information to Provide Accurate Information

(1) Prohibition

(A) *Reporting information with actual knowledge of errors.* A person shall not furnish any information relating to a consumer to any consumer reporting agency if the person knows or has reasonable cause to believe that the information is inaccurate.

(B) *Reporting information after notice and confirmation of errors.* A person shall not furnish information relating to a consumer to any consumer reporting agency if

(i) the person has been notified by the consumer, at the address specified by the person for such notices, that specific information is inaccurate; and

(ii) the information is, in fact, inaccurate.

(C) *No address requirement.* A person who clearly and conspicuously specifies to the consumer an address for notices referred to in subparagraph (B) shall not be subject to subparagraph (A); however, nothing in subparagraph (B) shall require a person to specify such an address.

(D) *Definition.* For purposes of subparagraph (A), the term "reasonable cause to believe that the information is inaccurate" means having specific knowledge, other than solely allegations by the consumer, that would cause a reasonable person to have substantial doubts about the accuracy of the information.

(2) *Duty to correct and update information.* A person who

(A) regularly and in the ordinary course of business furnishes information to one or more consumer reporting agencies about the person's transactions or experiences with any consumer; and

(B) has furnished to a consumer reporting agency information that the person determines is not complete or accurate, shall promptly notify the consumer reporting agency of that determination and provide to the agency any corrections to that information, or any additional information, that is necessary to make the information provided by the person to the agency complete and accurate, and shall not thereafter furnish to the agency any of the information that remains not complete or accurate.

(3) *Duty to provide notice of dispute.* If the completeness or accuracy of any information furnished by any person to any consumer reporting agency is disputed to such person by a consumer, the person may not furnish the information to any consumer reporting agency without notice that such information is disputed by the consumer.

(4) *Duty to provide notice of closed accounts.* A person who regularly and in the ordinary course of business furnishes information to a consumer reporting agency regarding a consumer who has a credit account with

that person shall notify the agency of the voluntary closure of the account by the consumer, in information regularly furnished for the period in which the account is closed.

(5) Duty to Provide Notice of Delinquency of Accounts

(A) *In general.* A person who furnishes information to a consumer reporting agency regarding a delinquent account being placed for collection, charged to profit or loss, or subjected to any similar action shall, not later than 90 days after furnishing the information, notify the agency of the date of delinquency on the account, which shall be the month and year of the commencement of the delinquency on the account that immediately preceded the action.

(B) *Rule of construction.* For purposes of this paragraph only, and provided that the consumer does not dispute the information, a person that furnishes information on a delinquent account that is placed for collection, charged for profit or loss, or subjected to any similar action, complies with this paragraph, if —

(i) the person reports the same date of delinquency as that provided by the creditor to which the account was owed at the time at which the commencement of the delinquency occurred, if the creditor previously reported that date of delinquency to a consumer reporting agency;

(ii) the creditor did not previously report the date of delinquency to a consumer reporting agency, and the person establishes and follows reasonable procedures to obtain the date of delinquency from the creditor or another reliable source and reports that date to a consumer reporting agency as the date of delinquency; or

(iii) the creditor did not previously report the date of delinquency to a consumer reporting agency and the date of delinquency cannot be reasonably obtained as provided in clause (ii), the person establishes and follows reasonable procedures to ensure the date reported as the date of delinquency precedes the date on which the account is placed for collection, charged to profit or loss, or subjected to any similar action, and reports such date to the credit reporting agency.

(6) Duties of Furnishers Upon Notice of Identity Theft-Related Information

(A) *Reasonable procedures.* A person that furnishes information to any consumer reporting agency shall have in place reasonable procedures to respond to any notification that it receives from a consumer reporting agency under section 605B relating to information resulting from identity theft, to prevent that person from refurnishing such blocked information.

(B) *Information alleged to result from identity theft.* If a consumer submits an identity theft report to a person who furnishes information to a consumer reporting agency at the address specified by that person for receiving such reports stating that information maintained by such person that purports to relate to the consumer resulted from identity theft, the person may not furnish such information that purports to relate to the consumer to any consumer reporting agency, unless the person subsequently knows or is informed by the consumer that the information is correct.

(7) Negative Information

(A) Notice to Consumer Required

(i) *In general.* If any financial institution that extends credit and regularly and in the ordinary course of business furnishes information to a consumer reporting agency described in section 603(p) furnishes negative information to such an agency regarding credit extended to a customer, the financial institution shall provide a notice of such furnishing of negative information, in writing, to the customer.

(ii) *Notice effective for subsequent submissions.* After providing such notice, the financial institution may submit additional negative information to a consumer reporting agency described in section 603(p) with respect to the same transaction, extension of credit, account, or customer without providing additional notice to the customer.

(B) Time of Notice

(i) *In general.* The notice required under subparagraph (A) shall be provided to the customer prior to, or no later than 30 days after, furnishing the negative information to a consumer reporting agency described in section 603(p).

(ii) *Coordination with new account disclosures.* If the notice is provided to the customer prior to furnishing the negative information to a consumer reporting agency, the notice may not be included in the initial disclosures provided under section 127(a) of the Truth in Lending Act.

(C) *Coordination with other disclosures.* The notice required under subparagraph (A)—

(i) may be included on or with any notice of default, any billing statement, or any other materials provided to the customer; and

(ii) must be clear and conspicuous.

(D) Model Disclosure

(i) *Duty of board to prepare.* The Board shall prescribe a brief model disclosure a financial institution may use to comply with subparagraph (A), which shall not exceed 30 words.

(ii) *Use of model not required.* No provision of this paragraph shall be construed as requiring a financial institution to use any such model form prescribed by the Board.

(iii) *Compliance using model.* A financial institution shall be deemed to be in compliance with subparagraph (A) if the financial institution uses any such model form prescribed by the Board, or the financial institution uses any such model form and rearranges its format.

(E) *Use of notice without submitting negative information.* No provision of this paragraph shall be construed as requiring a financial institution that has provided a customer with a notice described in subparagraph (A) to furnish negative information about the customer to a consumer reporting agency.

(F) *Safe harbor.* A financial institution shall not be liable for failure to perform the duties required by this paragraph if, at the time of the failure, the financial institution maintained reasonable policies and procedures to comply with this paragraph or the financial institution reasonably believed that the institution is prohibited, by law, from contacting the consumer.

(G) *Definitions.* For purposes of this paragraph, the following definitions shall apply:

(i) The term "negative information" means information concerning a customer's delinquencies, late payments, insolvency, or any form of default.

(ii) The terms "customer" and "financial institution" have the same meanings as in section 509 Public Law 106-102.

(8) Ability of Consumer to Dispute Information Directly with Furnisher

(A) *In general.* The Federal banking agencies, the National Credit Union Administration, and the Commission shall jointly prescribe regulations that shall identify the circumstances under which a furnisher shall be required to reinvestigate a dispute concerning the accuracy of information contained in a consumer report on the consumer, based on a direct request of a consumer.

(B) *Considerations.* In prescribing regulations under subparagraph (A), the agencies shall weigh—

(i) the benefits to consumers with the costs on furnishers and the credit reporting system;

(ii) the impact on the overall accuracy and integrity of consumer reports of any such requirements;

(iii) whether direct contact by the consumer with the furnisher would likely result in the most expeditious resolution of any such dispute; and

(iv) the potential impact on the credit reporting process if credit repair organizations, as defined in section 403(3) [15 U.S.C. $1679a(3)], including entities that would be a credit repair organization, but for section 403(3)(B)(i), are able to circumvent the prohibition in subparagraph (G).

(C) *Applicability.* Subparagraphs (D) through (G) shall apply in any circumstance identified under the regulations promulgated under subparagraph (A).

(D) *Submitting a notice of dispute.* A consumer who seeks to dispute the accuracy of information shall provide a dispute notice directly to such person at the address specified by the person for such notices that—

(i) identifies the specific information that is being disputed;

(ii) explains the basis for the dispute; and

(iii) includes all supporting documentation required by the furnisher to substantiate the basis of the dispute.

(E) *Duty of person after receiving notice of dispute.* After receiving a notice of dispute from a consumer pursuant to subparagraph (D), the person that provided the information in dispute to a consumer reporting agency shall—

(i) conduct an investigation with respect to the disputed information;

(ii) review all relevant information provided by the consumer with the notice;

(iii) complete such person's investigation of the dispute and report the results of the investigation to the consumer before the expiration of the period under section 611(a)(l) within which a consumer reporting agency would be required to complete its action if the consumer had elected to dispute the information under that section; and

(iv) if the investigation finds that the information reported was inaccurate, promptly notify each consumer reporting agency to which the person furnished the inaccurate information of that determination and provide to the agency any correction to that information that is necessary to make the information provided by the person accurate.

(F) Frivolous or Irrelevant Dispute

(i) *In general.* This paragraph shall not apply if the person receiving a notice of a dispute from a consumer reasonably determines that the dispute is frivolous or irrelevant, including—

(I) by reason of the failure of a consumer to provide sufficient information to investigate the disputed information; or

(II) the submission by a consumer of a dispute that is substantially the same as a dispute previously submitted by or for the consumer, either directly to the person or through a consumer reporting agency under subsection (b), with respect to which the person has already performed the person's duties under this paragraph or subsection (b), as applicable.

(ii) *Notice of determination.* Upon making any determination under clause

(i) that a dispute is frivolous or irrelevant, the person shall notify the consumer of such determination not later than 5 business days after making such determination, by mail or, if authorized by the consumer for that purpose, by any other means available to the person.

(iii) *Contents of notice.* A notice under clause (ii) shall include—

(I) the reasons for the determination under clause (i); and

(II) identification of any information required to investigate the disputed information, which may consist of a standardized form describing the general nature of such information.

(G) *Exclusion of credit repair organizations.* This paragraph shall not apply if the notice of the dispute is submitted by, is prepared on behalf of the consumer by, or is submitted on a form supplied to the consumer by, a credit repair organization, as defined in section 403(3), or an entity that would be a credit repair organization, but for section 403(3)(B)(i).

(9) *Duty to provide notice of status as medical information furnisher.* A person whose primary business is providing medical services, products, or devices, or the person's agent or assignee, who furnishes information to a consumer reporting agency on a consumer shall be considered a medical information furnisher for purposes of this title, and shall notify the agency of such status.

(b) Duties of Furnishers of Information upon Notice of Dispute

(1) *In general.* After receiving notice pursuant to section 611(a)(2) [§ 1681i] of a dispute with regard to the completeness or accuracy of any information provided by a person to a consumer reporting agency, the person shall

(A) conduct an investigation with respect to the disputed information;

(B) review all relevant information provided by the consumer reporting agency pursuant to section 611(a)(2) [§ 1681i];

(C) report the results of the investigation to the consumer reporting agency;

(D) if the investigation finds that the information is incomplete or inaccurate, report those results to all other consumer reporting agencies to which the person furnished the information and that compile and maintain files on consumers on a nationwide basis; and

(E) if an item of information disputed by a consumer is found to be inaccurate or incomplete or cannot be verified after any reinvestigation under paragraph (1), for purposes of reporting to a consumer reporting agency only, as appropriate, based on the results of the reinvestigation promptly—

(i) modify that item of information;

(ii) delete that item of information; or

(iii) permanently block the reporting of that item of information.

(2) *Deadline.* A person shall complete all investigations, reviews, and reports required under paragraph (1) regarding information provided by the person to a consumer reporting agency, before the expiration of the period under section 611(a)(l) [§ 1681i] within which the consumer reporting agency is required to complete actions required by that section regarding that information.

(c) *Limitation on liability.* Except as provided in section 621(c)(1)(B), sections 616 and 617 do not apply to any violation of—

(1) subsection (a) of this section, including any regulations issued thereunder;

(2) subsection (e) of this section, except that nothing in this paragraph shall limit, expand, or otherwise affect liability under section 616 or 617, as applicable, for violations of subsection (b) of this section; or

(3) subsection (e) of section 615.

(d) *Limitation on enforcement.* The provisions of law described in paragraphs (1) through (3) of subsection (c) (other than with respect to the exception described in paragraph (2) of subsection (c)) shall be enforced exclusively as provided under section 621 by the Federal agencies and officials and the State officials identified in section 621.

(e) Accuracy Guidelines and Regulations Required

(1) *Guidelines.* The Federal banking agencies, the National Credit Union Administration, and the Commission shall, with respect to the entities that are subject to their respective enforcement authority under section 621, and in coordination as described in paragraph (2)—

(A) establish and maintain guidelines for use by each person that furnishes information to a consumer reporting agency regarding the accuracy and integrity of the information relating to consumers that such entities furnish to consumer reporting agencies, and update such guidelines as often as necessary; and

(B) prescribe regulations requiring each person that furnishes information to a consumer reporting agency to establish reasonable policies and procedures for implementing the guidelines established pursuant to subparagraph (A).

(2) *Coordination.* Each agency required to prescribe regulations under paragraph (1) shall consult and coordinate with each other such agency so that, to the extent possible, the regulations prescribed by each such entity are consistent and comparable with the regulations prescribed by each other such agency.

(3) *Criteria.* In developing the guidelines required by paragraph (1)(A), the agencies described in paragraph (1) shall—

(A) identify patterns, practices, and specific forms of activity that can compromise the accuracy and integrity of information furnished to consumer reporting agencies;

(B) review the methods (including technological means) used to furnish information relating to consumers to consumer reporting agencies;

(C) determine whether persons that furnish information to consumer reporting agencies maintain and enforce policies to assure the accuracy and integrity of information furnished to consumer reporting agencies; and

(D) examine the policies and processes that persons that furnish information to consumer reporting agencies employ to conduct reinvestigations and correct inaccurate information relating to consumers that has been furnished to consumer reporting agencies.

[omitted Section 624. Affiliate sharing]

[omitted Section 625. Relation to State laws]

[omitted Section 626. Disclosures to FBI for counterintelligence purposes]

[omitted Section 627. Disclosures to governmental agencies for counterterrorism purposes]

Appendix VI

FAIR DEBT COLLECTION PRACTICES ACT

You'll appreciate the FDCPA if there's a collection agency harassing you. It's quite specific about what kind of collection tactics are illegal.

THE FAIR DEBT COLLECTION PRACTICES ACT
As amended by Public Law 104-208, 110 Stat. 3009 (Sept. 30, 1996)

To amend the Consumer Credit Protection Act to prohibit abusive practices by debt collectors.

TITLE VIII—DEBT COLLECTION PRACTICES [Fair Debt Collection Practices Act]

§ 802. Congressional findings and declarations of purpose [15 USC 1692]

(a) There is abundant evidence of the use of abusive, deceptive, and unfair debt collection practices by many debt collectors. Abusive debt collection practices contribute to the number of personal bankruptcies, to marital instability, to the loss of jobs, and to invasions of individual privacy.

(b) Existing laws and procedures for redressing these injuries are inadequate to protect consumers.

(c) Means other than misrepresentation or other abusive debt collection practices are available for the effective collection of debts.

(d) Abusive debt collection practices are carried on to a substantial extent in interstate commerce and through means and instrumentalities of such commerce. Even where abusive debt collection practices are purely intrastate in character, they nevertheless directly affect interstate commerce.

(e) It is the purpose of this title to eliminate abusive debt collection practices by debt collectors, to insure that those debt collectors who refrain from using abusive debt collection practices are not competitively disadvantaged, and to promote consistent State action to protect consumers against debt collection abuses.

§ 803. Definitions [15 USC 1692a]

As used in this title—

(1) The term "Commission" means the Federal Trade Commission.

(2) The term "communication" means the conveying of information regarding a debt directly or indirectly to any person through any medium.

(3) The term "consumer" means any natural person obligated or allegedly obligated to pay any debt.

(4) The term "creditor" means any person who offers or extends credit creating a debt or to whom a debt is owed, but such term does not include any person to the extent that he receives an assignment or transfer of a debt in default solely for the purpose of facilitating collection of such debt for another.

(5) The term "debt" means any obligation or alleged obligation of a consumer to pay money arising out of a transaction in which the money, property, insurance or services which are the subject of the transaction are primarily for personal, family, or household purposes, whether or not such obligation has been reduced to judgment.

(6) The term "debt collector" means any person who uses any instrumentality of interstate commerce or the mails in any business the principal purpose of which is the collection of any debts, or who regularly collects or attempts to collect, directly or indirectly, debts owed or due or asserted to be owed or due another. Notwithstanding the exclusion provided by clause (F) of the last sentence of this paragraph, the term includes any creditor who, in the process of collecting his own debts, uses any name other than his own which would indicate that a third person is collecting or attempting to collect such debts. For the purpose of section 808(6), such term also includes any person who uses any instrumentality of interstate commerce or the mails in any business the principal purpose of which is the enforcement of security interests. The term does not include—

(A) any officer or employee of a creditor while, in the name of the creditor, collecting debts for such creditor;

(B) any person while acting as a debt collector for another person, both of whom are related by common ownership or affiliated by corporate control, if the person acting as a debt collector does so only for persons to whom it is so related or affiliated and if the principal business of such person is not the collection of debts;

(C) any officer or employee of the United States or any State to the extent that collecting or attempting to collect any debt is in the performance of his official duties;

(D) any person while serving or attempting to serve legal process on any other person in connection with the judicial enforcement of any debt;

(E) any nonprofit organization which, at the request of consumers, performs bona fide consumer credit counseling and assists consumers in the liquidation of their debts by receiving payments from such consumers and distributing such amounts to creditors; and

(F) any person collecting or attempting to collect any debt owed or due or asserted to be owed or due another to the extent such activity (i) is incidental to a bona fide fiduciary obligation or a bona fide escrow arrangement; (ii) concerns a debt which was originated by such person; (iii) concerns a debt which was not in default at the time it was obtained by such person; or (iv) concerns a debt obtained by such person as a secured party in a commercial credit transaction involving the creditor.

(7) The term "location information" means a consumer's place of abode and his telephone number at such place, or his place of employment.

(8) The term "State" means any State, territory, or possession of the United States, the District of Columbia, the Commonwealth of Puerto Rico, or any political subdivision of any of the foregoing.

§ 804. Acquisition of location information [15 USC 1692b]

Any debt collector communicating with any person other than the consumer for the purpose of acquiring location information about the consumer shall—

(1) identify himself, state that he is confirming or correcting location information concerning the consumer, and, only if expressly requested, identify his employer;

(2) not state that such consumer owes any debt;

(3) not communicate with any such person more than once unless requested to do so by such person or unless the debt collector reasonably believes that the earlier response of such person is erroneous or incomplete and that such person now has correct or complete location information;

(4) not communicate by post card;

(5) not use any language or symbol on any envelope or in the con-

tents of any communication effected by the mails or telegram that indicates that the debt collector is in the debt collection business or that the communication relates to the collection of a debt; and

(6) after the debt collector knows the consumer is represented by an attorney with regard to the subject debt and has knowledge of, or can readily ascertain, such attorney's name and address, not communicate with any person other than that attorney, unless the attorney fails to respond within a reasonable period of time to the communication from the debt collector.

§ 805. Communication in connection with debt collection [15 USC 1692c]

(a) COMMUNICATION WITH THE CONSUMER GENERALLY. Without the prior consent of the consumer given directly to the debt collector or the express permission of a court of competent jurisdiction, a debt collector may not communicate with a consumer in connection with the collection of any debt—

(1) at any unusual time or place or a time or place known or which should be known to be inconvenient to the consumer. In the absence of knowledge of circumstances to the contrary, a debt collector shall assume that the convenient time for communicating with a consumer is after 8 o'clock antimeridian and before 9 o'clock postmeridian, local time at the consumer's location;

(2) if the debt collector knows the consumer is represented by an attorney with respect to such debt and has knowledge of, or can readily ascertain, such attorney's name and address, unless the attorney fails to respond within a reasonable period of time to a communication from the debt collector or unless the attorney consents to direct communication with the consumer; or

(3) at the consumer's place of employment if the debt collector knows or has reason to know that the consumer's employer prohibits the consumer from receiving such communication.

(b) COMMUNICATION WITH THIRD PARTIES. Except as provided in section 804, without the prior consent of the consumer given directly to the debt collector, or the express permission of a court of competent jurisdiction, or as reasonably necessary to effectuate a postjudgment judicial remedy, a debt collector may not communicate, in connection with the collection of any debt, with any person other than a consumer, his attorney, a consumer reporting agency if otherwise permitted by law, the creditor, the attorney of the creditor, or the attorney of the debt collector.

(c) CEASING COMMUNICATION. If a consumer notifies a debt collector in writing that the consumer refuses to pay a debt or that the consumer wishes the debt collector to cease further communication with the consumer, the debt collector shall not communicate further with the consumer with respect to such debt, except—

(1) to advise the consumer that the debt collector's further efforts are being terminated;

(2) to notify the consumer that the debt collector or creditor may invoke specified remedies which are ordinarily invoked by such debt collector or creditor; or

(3) where applicable, to notify the consumer that the debt collector or creditor intends to invoke a specified remedy.

If such notice from the consumer is made by mail, notification shall be complete upon receipt.

(d) For the purpose of this section, the term "consumer" includes the consumer's spouse, parent (if the consumer is a minor), guardian, executor, or administrator.

§ 806. Harassment or abuse [15 USC 1692d]

A debt collector may not engage in any conduct the natural consequence of which is to harass, oppress, or abuse any person in connection with the collection of a debt. Without limiting the general application of the foregoing, the following conduct is a violation of this section:

(1) The use or threat of use of violence or other criminal means to harm the physical person, reputation, or property of any person.

(2) The use of obscene or profane language or language the natural consequence of which is to abuse the hearer or reader.

(3) The publication of a list of consumers who allegedly refuse to pay debts, except to a consumer reporting agency or to persons meeting the requirements of section 603(f) or 604(3) of this Act.

(4) The advertisement for sale of any debt to coerce payment of the debt.

(5) Causing a telephone to ring or engaging any person in telephone conversation repeatedly or continuously with intent to annoy, abuse, or harass any person at the called number.

(6) Except as provided in section 804, the placement of telephone calls without meaningful disclosure of the caller's identity.

§ 807. False or misleading representations [15 USC 1692e]

A debt collector may not use any false, deceptive, or misleading representation or means in connection with the collection of any debt. Without limiting the general application of the foregoing, the following conduct is a violation of this section:

(1) The false representation or implication that the debt collector is vouched for, bonded by, or affiliated with the United States or any State,

including the use of any badge, uniform, or facsimile thereof.

(2) The false representation of —

(A) the character, amount, or legal status of any debt; or

(B) any services rendered or compensation which may be lawfully received by any debt collector for the collection of a debt.

(3) The false representation or implication that any individual is an attorney or that any communication is from an attorney.

(4) The representation or implication that nonpayment of any debt will result in the arrest or imprisonment of any person or the seizure, garnishment, attachment, or sale of any property or wages of any person unless such action is lawful and the debt collector or creditor intends to take such action.

(5) The threat to take any action that cannot legally be taken or that is not intended to be taken.

(6) The false representation or implication that a sale, referral, or other transfer of any interest in a debt shall cause the consumer to—

(A) lose any claim or defense to payment of the debt; or

(B) become subject to any practice prohibited by this title.

(7) The false representation or implication that the consumer committed any crime or other conduct in order to disgrace the consumer.

(8) Communicating or threatening to communicate to any person credit information which is known or which should be known to be false, including the failure to communicate that a disputed debt is disputed.

(9) The use or distribution of any written communication which simulates or is falsely represented to be a document authorized, issued, or approved by any court, official, or agency of the United States or any State, or which creates a false impression as to its source, authorization, or approval.

(10) The use of any false representation or deceptive means to collect or attempt to collect any debt or to obtain information concerning a consumer.

(11) The failure to disclose in the initial written communication with the consumer and, in addition, if the initial communication with the consumer is oral, in that initial oral communication, that the debt collector is attempting to collect a debt and that any information obtained will be used for that purpose, and the failure to disclose in subsequent communications that the communication is from a debt collector, except that this paragraph shall not apply to a formal pleading made in connection with a legal action.

(12) The false representation or implication that accounts have been turned over to innocent purchasers for value.

(13) The false representation or implication that documents are legal process.

(14) The use of any business, company, or organization name other

than the true name of the debt collector's business, company, or organization.

(15) The false representation or implication that documents are not legal process forms or do not require action by the consumer.

(16) The false representation or implication that a debt collector operates or is employed by a consumer reporting agency as defined by section 603(f) of this Act.

§ 808. Unfair practices [15 USC 1692f]

A debt collector may not use unfair or unconscionable means to collect or attempt to collect any debt. Without limiting the general application of the foregoing, the following conduct is a violation of this section:

(1) The collection of any amount (including any interest, fee, charge, or expense incidental to the principal obligation) unless such amount is expressly authorized by the agreement creating the debt or permitted by law.

(2) The acceptance by a debt collector from any person of a check or other payment instrument postdated by more than five days unless such person is notified in writing of the debt collector's intent to deposit such check or instrument not more than ten nor less than three business days prior to such deposit.

(3) The solicitation by a debt collector of any postdated check or other postdated payment instrument for the purpose of threatening or instituting criminal prosecution.

(4) Depositing or threatening to deposit any postdated check or other postdated payment instrument prior to the date on such check or instrument.

(5) Causing charges to be made to any person for communications by concealment of the true propose of the communication. Such charges include, but are not limited to, collect telephone calls and telegram fees.

(6) Taking or threatening to take any nonjudicial action to effect dispossession or disablement of property if —

(A) there is no present right to possession of the property claimed as collateral through an enforceable security interest;

(B) there is no present intention to take possession of the property; or

(C) the property is exempt by law from such dispossession or disablement.

(7) Communicating with a consumer regarding a debt by post card.

(8) Using any language or symbol, other than the debt collector's address, on any envelope when communicating with a consumer by use of the mails or by telegram, except that a debt collector may use his business name if such name does not indicate that he is in the debt collection business.

§ 809. Validation of debts [15 USC 1692g]

(a) Within five days after the initial communication with a consumer in connection with the collection of any debt, a debt collector shall, unless the following information is contained in the initial communication or the consumer has paid the debt, send the consumer a written notice containing—

(1) the amount of the debt;

(2) the name of the creditor to whom the debt is owed;

(3) a statement that unless the consumer, within thirty days after receipt of the notice, disputes the validity of the debt, or any portion thereof, the debt will be assumed to be valid by the debt collector;

(4) a statement that if the consumer notifies the debt collector in writing within the thirty-day period that the debt, or any portion thereof, is disputed, the debt collector will obtain verification of the debt or a copy of a judgment against the consumer and a copy of such verification or judgment will be mailed to the consumer by the debt collector; and

(5) a statement that, upon the consumer's written request within the thirty-day period, the debt collector will provide the consumer with the name and address of the original creditor, if different from the current creditor.

(b) If the consumer notifies the debt collector in writing within the thirty-day period described in subsection

(a) that the debt, or any portion thereof, is disputed, or that the consumer requests the name and address of the original creditor, the debt collector shall cease collection of the debt, or any disputed portion thereof, until the debt collector obtains verification of the debt or any copy of a judgment, or the name and address of the original creditor, and a copy of such verification or judgment, or name and address of the original creditor, is mailed to the consumer by the debt collector.

(c) The failure of a consumer to dispute the validity of a debt under this section may not be construed by any court as an admission of liability by the consumer.

§ 810. Multiple debts [15 USC 1692h]

If any consumer owes multiple debts and makes any single payment to any debt collector with respect to such debts, such debt collector may not apply such payment to any debt which is disputed by the consumer and, where applicable, shall apply such payment in accordance with the consumer's directions.

§ 811. Legal actions by debt collectors [15 USC 1692i]

(a) Any debt collector who brings any legal action on a debt against any consumer shall—

(1) in the case of an action to enforce an interest in real property securing the consumer's obligation, bring such action only in a judicial district or similar legal entity in which such real property is located; or

(2) in the case of an action not described in paragraph (1), bring such action only in the judicial district or similar legal entity—

(A) in which such consumer signed the contract sued upon; or

(B) in which such consumer resides at the commencement of the action.

(b) Nothing in this title shall be construed to authorize the bringing of legal actions by debt collectors.

§ 812. Furnishing certain deceptive forms [15 USC 1692j]

(a) It is unlawful to design, compile, and furnish any form knowing that such form would be used to create the false belief in a consumer that a person other than the creditor of such consumer is participating in the collection of or in an attempt to collect a debt such consumer allegedly owes such creditor, when in fact such person is not so participating.

(b) Any person who violates this section shall be liable to the same extent and in the same manner as a debt collector is liable under section 813 for failure to comply with a provision of this title.

§ 813. Civil liability [15 USC 1692k]

(a) Except as otherwise provided by this section, any debt collector who fails to comply with any provision of this title with respect to any person is liable to such person in an amount equal to the sum of—

(1) any actual damage sustained by such person as a result of such failure;

(2) (A) in the case of any action by an individual, such additional damages as the court may allow, but not exceeding $1,000; or

(B) in the case of a class action, (i) such amount for each named plaintiff as could be recovered under subparagraph (A), and (ii) such amount as the court may allow for all other class members, without regard to a minimum individual recovery, not to exceed the lesser of $500,000 or 1 per centum of the net worth of the debt collector; and

(3) in the case of any successful action to enforce the foregoing liability, the costs of the action, together with a reasonable attorney's fee as determined by the court. On a finding by the court that an action under this section was brought in bad faith and for the purpose of harassment, the court may award to the defendant attorney's fees reasonable in relation to the work expended and costs.

(b) In determining the amount of liability in any action under subsection (a), the court shall consider, among other relevant factors—

(1) in any individual action under subsection (a)(2)(A), the fre-

quency and persistence of noncompliance by the debt collector, the nature of such noncompliance, and the extent to which such noncompliance was intentional; or

(2) in any class action under subsection (a)(2)(B), the frequency and persistence of noncompliance by the debt collector, the nature of such noncompliance, the resources of the debt collector, the number of persons adversely affected, and the extent to which the debt collector's noncompliance was intentional.

(c) A debt collector may not be held liable in any action brought under this title if the debt collector shows by a preponderance of evidence that the violation was not intentional and resulted from a bona fide error notwithstanding the maintenance of procedures reasonably adapted to avoid any such error.

(d) An action to enforce any liability created by this title may be brought in any appropriate United States district court without regard to the amount in controversy, or in any other court of competent jurisdiction, within one year from the date on which the violation occurs.

(e) No provision of this section imposing any liability shall apply to any act done or omitted in good faith in conformity with any advisory opinion of the Commission, notwithstanding that after such act or omission has occurred, such opinion is amended, rescinded, or determined by judicial or other authority to be invalid for any reason.

§ 814. Administrative enforcement [15 USC 1692l]

(a) Compliance with this title shall be enforced by the Commission, except to the extend that enforcement of the requirements imposed under this title is specifically committed to another agency under subsection (b). For purpose of the exercise by the Commission of its functions and powers under the Federal Trade Commission Act, a violation of this title shall be deemed an unfair or deceptive act or practice in violation of that Act. All of the functions and powers of the Commission under the Federal Trade Commission Act are available to the Commission to enforce compliance by any person with this title, irrespective of whether that person is engaged in commerce or meets any other jurisdictional tests in the Federal Trade Commission Act, including the power to enforce the provisions of this title in the same manner as if the violation had been a violation of a Federal Trade Commission trade regulation rule.

(b) Compliance with any requirements imposed under this title shall be enforced under—

(1) section 8 of the Federal Deposit Insurance Act, in the case of—

(A) national banks, by the Comptroller of the Currency;

(B) member banks of the Federal Reserve System (other than national banks), by the Federal Reserve Board; and

(C) banks the deposits or accounts of which are insured by the Federal Deposit Insurance Corporation (other than members of the Federal Reserve System), by the Board of Directors of the Federal Deposit Insurance Corporation;

(2) section 5(d) of the Home Owners Loan Act of 1933, section 407 of the National Housing Act, and sections 6(i) and 17 of the Federal Home Loan Bank Act, by the Federal Home Loan Bank Board (acting directing or through the Federal Savings and Loan Insurance Corporation), in the case of any institution subject to any of those provisions;

(3) the Federal Credit Union Act, by the Administrator of the National Credit Union Administration with respect to any Federal credit union;

(4) subtitle IV of Title 49, by the Interstate Commerce Commission with respect to any common carrier subject to such subtitle;

(5) the Federal Aviation Act of 1958, by the Secretary of Transportation with respect to any air carrier or any foreign air carrier subject to that Act; and

(6) the Packers and Stockyards Act, 1921 (except as provided in section 406 of that Act), by the Secretary of Agriculture with respect to any activities subject to that Act.

(c) For the purpose of the exercise by any agency referred to in subsection (b) of its powers under any Act referred to in that subsection, a violation of any requirement imposed under this title shall be deemed to be a violation of a requirement imposed under that Act. In addition to its powers under any provision of law specifically referred to in subsection (b), each of the agencies referred to in that subsection may exercise, for the purpose of enforcing compliance with any requirement imposed under this title any other authority conferred on it by law, except as provided in subsection (d).

(d) Neither the Commission nor any other agency referred to in subsection (b) may promulgate trade regulation rules or other regulations with respect to the collection of debts by debt collectors as defined in this title.

§ 815. Reports to Congress by the Commission [15 USC 1692m]

(a) Not later than one year after the effective date of this title and at one-year intervals thereafter, the Commission shall make reports to the Congress concerning the administration of its functions under this title, including such recommendations as the Commission deems necessary or appropriate. In addition, each report of the Commission shall include its assessment of the extent to which compliance with this title is being achieved and a summary of the enforcement actions taken by the Commission under section 814 of this title.

(b) In the exercise of its functions under this title, the Commission may obtain upon request the views of any other Federal agency which exercises enforcement functions under section 814 of this title.

§ 816. Relation to State laws [15 USC 1692n]

This title does not annul, alter, or affect, or exempt any person subject to the provisions of this title from complying with the laws of any State with respect to debt collection practices, except to the extent that those laws are inconsistent with any provision of this title, and then only to the extent of the inconsistency. For purposes of this section, a State law is not inconsistent with this title if the protection such law affords any consumer is greater than the protection provided by this title.

§ 817. Exemption for State regulation [15 USC 1692o]

The Commission shall by regulation exempt from the requirements of this title any class of debt collection practices within any State if the Commission determines that under the law of that State that class of debt collection practices is subject to requirements substantially similar to those imposed by this title, and that there is adequate provision for enforcement.

§ 818. Effective date [15 USC 1692 note]

This title takes effect upon the expiration of six months after the date of its enactment, but section 809 shall apply only with respect to debts for which the initial attempt to collect occurs after such effective date.
Approved September 20, 1997

Appendix VII

FAIR CREDIT BILLING ACT (FCBA)

The FCBA is key to many of the dispute tactics in this book, because it puts a burden on many creditors to bill you in a certain manner before a debt can be considered late. In many situations, it protects you from being considered late in payment if you contest part of a bill.

TITLE III—FAIR CREDIT BILLING

"Sec. 301. Short title

This title may be cited as the "Fair Credit Billing Act."

"Sec. 302. Declaration of purpose

The last sentence of section 102 of the Truth in Lending Act (15 U.S.C. 1601) is amended by striking out the period and inserting in lieu thereof a comma and the following : "and to protect the consumer against inaccurate and unfair credit billing and credit card practices."

"Sec. 303. Definitions of creditor and open end credit plan

The first sentence of section 103 (f) of the Truth in Lending Act (15 U.S.C. 1602 (f)) is amended to read as follows: "The term 'creditor' refers only to creditors who regularly extend, or arrange for the extension of, credit which is payable by agreement in more than four installments or for which the payment of a finance charge is or may be required, whether in connection with loans, sales of property or services, or otherwise. For the purposes of the requirements imposed under Chapter 4 and sections 127 (a)(6), 127 (a)(7), 127 (a)(8), 127 (b)(1), 127 (b)(2), 127 (b)(3), 127 (b)(9), and 127 (b)(11) of Chapter 2 of this Title, the term 'creditor' shall also include card issuers whether or not the amount due is payable by agreement in more than four installments or the payment of a finance charge is or may be required, and the Board shall, by regulation, apply these requirements to such card issuers, to the extent appropriate, even though the requirements are by their terms applicable only to creditors offering open end credit plans.

"Sec. 304. Disclosure of fair credit billing rights

"(a) Section 127 (a) of the Truth in Lending Act (15 U.S.C. 1637 (a)) is amended by adding at the end thereof a new paragraph as follows:

"(8) A statement, in a form prescribed by regulations of the Board of the protection provided by sections 161 and 170 to an obligor and the creditor's responsibilities under sections 162 and 170. With respect to each of two billing cycles per year, at semiannual intervals, the creditor shall transmit such statement to each obligor to whom the creditor is required to transmit a statement pursuant to section 127 (b) for such billing cycle."

"(b) Section 127 (c) of such Act (15 U.S.C. 1637 (c)) is amended to read:

"(c) In the case of any existing account under an open end consumer credit plan having an outstanding balance of more than $1 at or after the close of the creditor's first full billing cycle under the plan after the effective date of subsection (a) or any amendments thereto, the items described in subsection (a), to the extent applicable and not previously disclosed, shall be disclosed in a notice mailed or delivered to the obligor not later than the time of mailing the next statement required by subsection (b)."

"Sec. 305. Disclosure of billing contact

Section 127 (b) of the Truth in Lending Act (15 U.S.C. 1637 (b)) is amended by adding at the end thereof a new paragraph as follows:

"(11) The address to be used by the creditor for the purpose of receiving billing inquiries from the obligor."

"Sec. 306. Billing practices

The Truth in Lending Act (15 U.S.C. 1601–1665) is amended by adding at the end thereof a new chapter as follows:

"Chapter 4—Credit Billing'

"Sec. 161. Correction of billing errors:

"(a) If a creditor, within sixty days after having transmitted to an obligor a statement of the obligor's account in connection with an extension of consumer credit, receives at the address disclosed under section 127 (b)(11) a written notice (other than notice on a payment stub or other payment medium supplied by the creditor if the creditor so stipulates with the disclosure required under section 127 (a)(8)) from the obligor in which the obligor—

"(1) sets forth or otherwise enables the creditor to identify the name and account number (if any) of the obligor,

"(2) indicates the obligor's belief that the statement contains a billing error and the amount of such billing error, and

"(3) sets forth the reasons for the obligor's belief (to the extent applicable) that the statement contains a billing error, the creditor shall, unless the obligor has, after giving such written notice and before the expiration of the time limits herein specified, agreed that the statement was correct—

"(A) not later than thirty days after the receipt of the notice, send a written acknowledgment thereof to the obligor, unless the action required in subparagraph (B) is taken within such thirty-day period, and

"(B) not later than two complete billing cycles of the creditor (in no event later than ninety days) after the receipt of the notice and prior to taking any action to collect the amount, or any part thereof, indicated by the obligor under paragraph (2) either—

"(i) make appropriate corrections in the account of this obligor, including the crediting of any finance charges on amounts erroneously billed, and transmit to the obligor a notification of such corrections and the creditor's explanation of any change in the amount indicated by the obligor under paragraph (2) and, if any such change is made and the obligor so requests, copies of documentary evidence of the obligor's indebtedness; or "(ii) send a written explanation or clarification to the obligor, after having conducted an investigation, setting forth to the extent applicable the reasons why the creditor believes the account of the obligor was correctly shown in the statement and, upon request of the obligor, provide copies of documentary evidence of the obligor's indebtedness. In the case of a billing error where the obligor alleges that the creditor's billing statement reflects goods not delivered to the obligor or his designee in accordance with the agreement made at the time of the transaction, a creditor may not construe such amount to be correctly shown unless he determines that such goods were actually delivered, mailed, or otherwise sent to the obligor and provides the obligor with a statement of such determination.

After complying with the provisions of this subsection with respect to an alleged billing error, a creditor has no further responsibility under this section if the obligor continues to make substantially the same allegation with respect to such error.

"(b) For the purpose of this section, a 'billing error' consists of any of the following:

"(1) A reflection on a statement of an extension of credit which was not made to the obligor or, if made, was not in the amount reflected on such statement.

"(2) A reflection on a statement of an extension of credit for which the obligor requests additional clarification including documentary evidence thereof.

"(3) A reflection on a statement of goods or services not accepted by the obligor or his designee or not delivered to the obligor or his designee in accordance with the agreement made at the time of a transaction.

"(4) The creditor's failure to reflect properly on a statement a payment made by the obligor or a credit issued to the obligor.

"(5) A computation error or similar error of an accounting nature of the creditor on a statement.

"(6) Any other error described in regulations of the Board. "(c) For the purposes of this section, 'action to collect the amount', or any part thereof, indicated by an obligor under paragraph (2) does not include the sending of statements of account to the obligor following written notice from the obligor as specified under subsection (a), if —

"(1) the obligor's account is not restricted or closed because of the failure of the obligor to pay the amount indicated under paragraph (2) of subsection (a), and

"(2) the creditor indicates the payment of such amount is not required pending the creditor's compliance with this section. Nothing in this section shall be construed to prohibit any action by a creditor to collect any amount which has not been indicated by the obligor to contain a billing error.

"(d) Pursuant to regulations of the Board, a creditor operating an open end consumer credit plan may not, prior to the sending of the written explanation or clarification required under paragraph (B) (ii), restrict or close an account with respect to which the obligor has indicated pursuant to subsection (a) that he believes such account to contain a billing error solely because of the obligor's failure to pay the amount indicated to be in error. Nothing in this subsection shall be deemed to prohibit a creditor from applying against the credit limit on the obligor's account the amount indicated to be in error.

"(e) Any creditor who fails to comply with the requirements of this section or section 162 forfeits any right to collect from the obligor the amount indicated by the obligor under paragraph (2) of subsection (a) of this section, and any finance charges thereon, except that the amount required to be forfeited under this subsection may not exceed $50.

"Sec. 162. Regulation of credit reports

"(a) After receiving a notice from an obligor as provided in section 161 (a), a creditor or his agent may not directly or indirectly threaten to report to any person adversely on the obligor's credit rating or credit standing because of the obligor's failure to pay the amount indicated by the obligor under section 161 (a)(2), and such amount may not be reported as delinquent to any third party until the creditor has met the requirements of section 161 and has allowed the obligor the same number of days (not less than ten) thereafter to make payment as is provided under the credit agreement with the obligor for the payment of undisputed amounts.

"(b) If a creditor receives a further written notice from an obligor that an amount is still in dispute within the time allowed for payment under subsection (a) of this section, a creditor may not report to any third party that the amount of the obligor is delinquent because the obligor has failed to pay an amount which he has indicated under section 161 (a)(2), unless the creditor also reports that the amount is in dispute and, at the same time, notifies the obligor of the name and address of each party to whom the creditor is reporting information concerning the delinquency.

"(c) A creditor shall report any subsequent resolution of any delinquencies reported pursuant to subsection (b) to the parties to whom such delinquencies were initially reported.

"Sec. 163. Length of billing period

"(a) If an open end consumer credit plan provides a time period within which an obligor may repay any portion of the credit extended without incurring an additional finance charge, such additional finance charge may not be imposed with respect to such portion of the credit extended for the billing cycle of which such period is a part unless a statement which includes the amount upon which the finance charge for that period is based was mailed at least fourteen days prior to the date specified in the statement by which payment must be made in order to avoid imposition of that finance charge.

"(b) Subsection (a) does not apply in any case where a creditor has been prevented, delayed, or hindered in making timely mailing or delivery of such periodic statement within the time period specified in such subsection because of an act of God, war, natural disaster, strike, or other excusable or justifiable cause, as determined under regulations of the Board.

"Sec. 164. Prompt crediting of payments

"Payments received from an obligor under an open end consumer credit plan by the creditor shall be posted promptly to the obligor's account as specified in regulations of the Board. Such regulations shall prevent a finance charge from being imposed on any obligor if the creditor has received the obligor's payment in readily identifiable form in the amount, manner, location, and time indicated by the credit to avoid the imposition thereof.

"Sec. 165. Crediting excess payments

"Whenever an obligor transmits funds to a creditor in excess of the total balance due on an open end consumer credit account, the creditor shall promptly (1) upon request of the obligor refund the amount of the overpayment, or (2) credit such amount to the obligor's account.

"Sec. 166. Prompt notification of returns

"With respect to any sales transaction where a credit card has been used to obtain credit, where the seller is a person other than the card issuer, and where the seller accepts or allows a return of the goods or forgiveness of a debit for services which were the subject of such sale, the seller shall promptly transmit to the credit card issuer, a credit statement with respect thereto and the credit card issuer shall credit the account of the obligor for the amount of the transaction.

"Sec. 167. Use of cash discounts

"(a) With respect to credit card which may be used for extensions of credit in sales transactions in which the seller is a person other than the card issuer; the card issuer may not, by contract or otherwise, prohibit any such seller from offering a discount to a cardholder to induce the cardholder to pay by cash, check, or similar means rather than use a credit card.

"(b) With respect to any sales transaction, and discount not in excess of 5 per centum offered by the seller for the purpose of inducing payment by cash, check, or other means not involving the use of a credit card shall not constitute a finance charge as determined under section 106, if such discount is offered to all prospective buyers and its availability is disclosed to all prospective buyers clearly and conspicuously in accordance with regulations of the Board.

"Sec. 168. Prohibition of tie-in services

"Notwithstanding any agreement to the contrary, a card issuer may not require a seller, as a condition to participating in a credit card plan, to open an account with or procure any other service from the card issuer or its subsidiary or agent.

"Sec. 169. Prohibition of offsets

"(a) A card issuer may not take any action to offset a cardholder's indebtedness arising in connection with a consumer credit transaction under the relevant credit card plan against funds of the cardholder held on deposit with the card issuer unless—

"(1) such action was previously authorized in writing by the cardholder in accordance with a credit plan whereby the cardholder agrees periodically to pay debts incurred in his open end credit account by permitting the card issuer periodically to deduct all or a portion of such debt from the cardholder's deposit account, and

"(2) such action with respect to any outstanding disputed amount not be taken by the card issuer upon request of the cardholder. In the case of any credit card account in existence on the effective date of this section, the previous written authorization referred to in clause (1) shall not be required until the date (after such effective date) when such account is renewed, but in no case later than one year after such effective date. Such written authorization shall be deemed to exist if the card issuer has previously notified the cardholder that the use of his credit card account will subject any funds which the card issuer holds in deposit accounts of such cardholder to offset against any amounts due and payable on his credit card account which have not been paid in accordance with the terms of the agreement between the card issuer and the cardholder.

"(b) This section does not alter or affect the right under State law of a card issuer to attach or otherwise levy upon funds of a cardholder held on deposit with the card issuer if that remedy is constitutionally available to creditors generally.

"Sec. 170. Rights of credit card customers

"(a) Subject to the limitation contained in subsection (b), a card issuer who has issued a credit card to a cardholder pursuant to an open end consumer credit plan shall be subject to all claims (other than tort claims) and defenses arising out of any transaction in which the credit card is used as a method of payment or extension of credit if (1) the obligor has made a good faith attempt to obtain satisfactory resolution of a disagreement or problem relative to the transaction from the person honoring the credit card; (2) the amount of the initial transaction exceeds $50; and (3) the place where the initial transaction occurred was in the same State as the mailing address previously provided by the cardholder or was within 100 miles from such address, except that the limitations set forth in clauses (2) and (3) with respect to an obligor's right to asset claims and defenses against a card issuer shall not be applicable to any transaction in which the person honoring the credit card (A) is the same person as the card issuer, (B) is controlled by the card issuer, (C) is under direct or indirect common control with the card issuer, (D) is a franchised dealer in the card issuer's products or services, or (E) has obtained the order for such transaction through a mail solicitation made by or participated in by the card issuer in which the cardholder is solicited to enter into such transaction by using the credit card issued by the card issuer.

"(b) The amount of claims or defenses asserted by the cardholder may not exceed the amount of credit outstanding with respect to such transaction at the time the cardholder first notifies the card issuer or the person honoring the credit card of such claim or defense. For the purpose of determining the amount of credit outstanding in the preceding sentence, payments and credits to the cardholder's account are deemed to have been applied, in the order indicated, to the payment of: (1) late charges in the order of their entry to the account; (2) finance charges in order of their entry to the account; and (3) debits to the account other than those set forth above, in the order in which each debit entry to the account was made.

"Sec. 171. Relation to State laws

"(a) This chapter does not annul, alter, or affect, or exempt any person subject to the provisions of this chapter from complying with, the laws of any State with respect to credit billing practices, except to the extent that those laws are inconsistent with any provision of this chapter, and then only to the extent of the inconsistency. The Board may not determine that any State law is inconsistent with any provision of this chapter if the Board determines that such law gives greater protection to the consumer.

"(b) The Board shall by regulation exempt from the requirements of this chapter any class of credit transactions within any State if it determines that under the law of that State that class of transactions is subject to requirements substantially similar to those imposed under this chapter or that such law gives greater protection to the consumer, and that there is adequate provision for enforcement."

Appendix VIII

TRUTH IN LENDING ACT (TILA)

The TILA helps spell out consumer rights in mortgages and leases. Truth in Lending focuses on issues such as finance charges, fees, and surcharges to credit transactions, as well as mandatory disclosures and consumers' rights to break contracts within three days of signing. If you think a lender has misrepresented information to you, consider consulting the Truth in Lending Act.

However, for the purposes of this book, most consumers will find the appropriate legal rights described in the Fair Credit Billing Act and the Fair Credit Reporting Act, included in earlier Appendixes of this book.

To read the Truth in Lending Act, go to http://www4.law. cornell.edu/uscode/html/uscode15/usc_sup_01_15_10_41.htm/

Or visit your library and ask for the reference book containing U.S. Code Title 15, Sections 1601 to 1615, 1631 to 1649, 1661 to 1667, 1671 to 1677, 1679, 1681, 1691 to 1693.

Appendix IX

CREDIT REPAIR ORGANIZATIONS ACT

The Credit Repair Organizations Act regulates how companies who offer consumer credit repair operate, including prohibiting deceptive advertising, limiting the promises such companies can make and their payment terms.

SEC. 402. FINDINGS AND PURPOSES.

(a) *Findings.* — The Congress makes the following findings:

(1) Consumers have a vital interest in establishing and maintaining their credit worthiness and credit standing in order to obtain and use credit. As a result, consumers who have experienced credit problems may seek assistance from credit repair organizations which offer to improve the credit standing of such consumers.

(2) Certain advertising and business practices of some companies engaged in the business of credit repair services have worked a financial

hardship upon consumers, particularly those of limited economic means and who are inexperienced in credit matters.

(b) *Purposes.*—The purposes of this title are—

(1) to ensure that prospective buyers of the services of credit repair organizations are provided with the information necessary to make an informed decision regarding the purchase of such services; and

(2) to protect the public from unfair or deceptive advertising and business practices by credit repair organizations.

SEC. 403. DEFINITIONS.

For purposes of this title, the following definitions apply:

(1) *Consumer.*—The term 'consumer' means an individual.

(2) *Consumer credit transaction.*—The term 'consumer credit transaction' means any transaction in which credit is offered or extended to an individual for personal, family, or household purposes.

(3) *Credit repair organization.*—The term 'credit repair organization'—

(A) means any person who uses any instrumentality of interstate commerce or the mails to sell, provide, or perform (or represent that such person can or will sell, provide, or perform) any service, in return for the payment of money or other valuable consideration, for the express or implied purpose of—

(i) improving any consumer's credit record, credit history, or credit rating; or

(ii) providing advice or assistance to any consumer with regard to any activity or service described in clause (i); and

(B) does not include—

(i) any nonprofit organization which is exempt from taxation under section 501(c)(3) of the Internal Revenue Code of 1986;

(ii) any creditor (as defined in section 103 of the Truth in Lending Act), with respect to any consumer, to the extent the creditor is assisting the consumer to restructure any debt owed by the consumer to the creditor; or

(iii) any depository institution (as that term is defined in section 3 of the Federal Deposit Insurance Act) or any Federal or State credit union (as those terms are defined in section 101 of the Federal Credit Union Act), or any affiliate or subsidiary of such a depository institution or credit union.

(4) *Credit.*—The term 'credit' has the meaning given to such term in section 103(e) of this Act.

SEC. 404. PROHIBITED PRACTICES.

(a) *In General.*—No person may—

(1) make any statement, or counsel or advise any consumer to make any statement, which is untrue or misleading (or which, upon the exercise of reasonable care, should be known by the credit repair organization, officer, employee, agent, or other person to be untrue or misleading) with respect to any consumer's credit worthiness, credit standing, or credit capacity to—

(A) any consumer reporting agency (as defined in section 603(f) of this Act); or

(B) any person—

(i) who has extended credit to the consumer; or

(ii) to whom the consumer has applied or is applying for an extension of credit;

(2) make any statement, or counsel or advise any consumer to make any statement, the intended effect of which is to alter the consumer's identification to prevent the display of the consumer's credit record, history, or rating for the purpose of concealing adverse information that is accurate and not obsolete to—

(A) any consumer reporting agency;

(B) any person—

(i) who has extended credit to the consumer; or

(ii) to whom the consumer has applied or is applying for an extension of credit;

(3) make or use any untrue or misleading representation of the services of the credit repair organization; or

(4) engage, directly or indirectly, in any act, practice, or course of business that constitutes or results in the commission of, or an attempt to commit, a fraud or deception on any person in connection with the offer or sale of the services of the credit repair organization.

(b) *Payment in Advance.*—No credit repair organization may charge or receive any money or other valuable consideration for the performance of any service which the credit repair organization has agreed to perform for any consumer before such service is fully performed.

SEC. 405. DISCLOSURES.

(a) *Disclosure Required.*—Any credit repair organization shall provide any consumer with the following written statement before any contract or agreement between the consumer and the credit repair organization is executed:

Consumer Credit File Rights Under State and Federal Law

You have a right to dispute inaccurate information in your credit report by contacting the credit bureau directly. However, neither you nor any "credit repair" company or credit repair organization has the right to have accurate, current, and verifiable information removed from your credit report. The credit bureau must remove accurate, negative information from your report only if it is over 7 years old. Bankruptcy information can be reported for 10 years.

You have a right to obtain a copy of your credit report from a credit bureau. You may be charged a reasonable fee. There is no fee, however, if you have been turned down for credit, employment, insurance, or a rental dwelling because of information in your credit report within the preceding 60 days. The credit bureau must provide someone to help you interpret the information in your credit file. You are entitled to receive a free copy of your credit report if you are unemployed and intend to apply for employment in the next 60 days, if you are a recipient of public welfare assistance, or if you have reason to believe that there is inaccurate information in your credit report due to fraud.

You have a right to sue a credit repair organization that violates the Credit Repair Organization Act. This law prohibits deceptive practices by credit repair organizations.

You have the right to cancel your contract with any credit repair organization for any reason within 3 business days from the date you signed it.

Credit bureaus are required to follow reasonable procedures to ensure that the information they report is accurate. However, mistakes may occur.

You may, on your own, notify a credit bureau in writing that you dispute the accuracy of information in your credit file. The credit bureau must then reinvestigate and modify or remove inaccurate or incomplete information. The credit bureau may not charge any fee for this service. Any pertinent information and copies of all documents you have concerning an error should be given to the credit bureau.

If the credit bureau's reinvestigation does not resolve the dispute to your satisfaction, you may send a brief statement to the credit bureau, to be kept in your file, explaining why you think the record is inaccurate. The credit bureau must include a summary of your statement about disputed information with any report it issues about you.

The Federal Trade Commission regulates credit bureaus and credit repair organizations. For more information contact:

The Public Reference Branch
Federal Trade Commission
Washington, D.C. 20580

(b) *Separate Statement Requirement.* — The written statement required under this section shall be provided as a document which is separate from any written contract or other agreement between the credit repair organization and the consumer or any other written material provided to the consumer.

(c) *Retention of Compliance Records.*—

(1) *In general.*—The credit repair organization shall maintain a copy of the statement signed by the consumer acknowledging receipt of the statement.

(2) *Maintenance for 2 years.*—The copy of any consumer's statement shall be maintained in the organization's files for 2 years after the date on which the statement is signed by the consumer.

SEC. 406. CREDIT REPAIR ORGANIZATIONS CONTRACTS.

(a) *Written Contracts Required.*—No services may be provided by any credit repair organization for any consumer—

(1) unless a written and dated contract (for the purchase of such services) which meets the requirements of subsection (b) has been signed by the consumer; or

(2) before the end of the 3-business-day period beginning on the date the contract is signed.

(b) *Terms and Conditions of Contract.*—No contract referred to in subsection (a) meets the requirements of this subsection unless such contract includes (in writing)—

(1) the terms and conditions of payment, including the total amount of all payments to be made by the consumer to the credit repair organization or to any other person;

(2) a full and detailed description of the services to be performed by the credit repair organization for the consumer, including—

(A) all guarantees of performance; and

(B) an estimate of—

(i) the date by which the performance of the services (to be performed by the credit repair organization or any other person) will be complete; or

(ii) the length of the period necessary to perform such services;

(3) the credit repair organization's name and principal business address; and

(4) a conspicuous statement in bold face type, in immediate proximity to the space reserved for the consumer's signature on the contract, which reads as follows: "You may cancel this contract without penalty or obligation at any time before midnight of the 3rd business day after the date on which you signed the contract. See the attached notice of cancellation form for an explanation of this right."

SEC. 407. RIGHT TO CANCEL CONTRACT.

(a) *In General.*—Any consumer may cancel any contract with any credit repair organization without penalty or obligation by notifying the credit repair organization of the consumer's intention to do so at any time before midnight of the 3rd business day which begins after the date on which the contract or agreement between the consumer and the credit repair organization is executed or would, but for this subsection, become enforceable against the parties.

(b) *Cancellation Form and Other Information.* — Each contract shall be accompanied by a form, in duplicate, which has the heading 'Notice of Cancellation' and contains in bold face type the following statement:

"You may cancel this contract, without any penalty or obligation, at any time before midnight of the 3rd day which begins after the date the contract is signed by you.

To cancel this contract, mail or deliver a signed, dated copy of this cancellation notice, or any other written notice to (name of credit repair organization) at (address of credit repair organization) before midnight on (date)

I hereby cancel this transaction,

(date)

(purchaser's signature)."

(c) *Consumer Copy of Contract Required.* — Any consumer who enters into any contract with any credit repair organization shall be given, by the organization —

(1) a copy of the completed contract and the disclosure statement required under section 405; and

(2) a copy of any other document the credit repair organization requires the consumer to sign, at the time the contract or the other document is signed.

SEC. 408. NONCOMPLIANCE WITH THIS TITLE.

(a) *Consumer Waivers Invalid.* — Any waiver by any consumer of any protection provided by or any right of the consumer under this title —

(1) shall be treated as void; and

(2) may not be enforced by any Federal or State court or any other person.

(b) *Attempt To Obtain Waiver.* — Any attempt by any person to obtain a waiver from any consumer of any protection provided by or any right of the consumer under this title shall be treated as a violation of this title.

(c) *Contracts Not in Compliance.* — Any contract for services which does not comply with the applicable provisions of this title —

(1) shall be treated as void; and

(2) may not be enforced by any Federal or State court or any other person.

SEC. 409. CIVIL LIABILITY.

(a) *Liability Established.*—Any person who fails to comply with any provision of this title with respect to any other person shall be liable to such person in an amount equal to the sum of the amounts determined under each of the following paragraphs:

(1) *Actual damages.*—The greater of—

(A) the amount of any actual damage sustained by such person as a result of such failure; or

(B) any amount paid by the person to the credit repair organization.

(2) *Punitive damages.*—

(A) *Individual actions.*—In the case of any action by an individual, such additional amount as the court may allow.

(B) *Class actions.*—In the case of a class action, the sum of—

(i) the aggregate of the amount which the court may allow for each named plaintiff; and

(ii) the aggregate of the amount which the court may allow for each other class member, without regard to any minimum individual recovery.

(3) *Attorneys' fees.*—In the case of any successful action to enforce any liability under paragraph (1) or (2), the costs of the action, together with reasonable attorneys' fees.

(b) *Factors to Be Considered in Awarding Punitive Damages.*—In determining the amount of any liability of any credit repair organization under subsection (a)(2), the court shall consider, among other relevant factors—

(1) the frequency and persistence of noncompliance by the credit repair organization;

(2) the nature of the noncompliance;

(3) the extent to which such noncompliance was intentional; and

(4) in the case of any class action, the number of consumers adversely affected.

SEC. 410. ADMINISTRATIVE ENFORCEMENT.

(a) *In General.*—Compliance with the requirements imposed under this title with respect to credit repair organizations shall be enforced under the Federal Trade Commission Act by the Federal Trade Commission.

(b) *Violations of This Title Treated as Violations of Federal Trade Commission Act.*—

(1) *In general.*—For the purpose of the exercise by the Federal Trade Commission of the Commission's functions and powers under the Federal Trade Commission Act, any violation of any requirement or prohibition imposed under this title with respect to credit repair organizations shall constitute an unfair or deceptive act or practice in commerce in violation of section 5(a) of the Federal Trade Commission Act.

(2) *Enforcement authority under other law.*—All functions and powers of the Federal Trade Commission under the Federal Trade Commission Act shall be available to the Commission to enforce compliance with this title by any person subject to enforcement by the Federal Trade Commission pursuant to this subsection, including the power to enforce the provisions of this title in the same manner as if the violation had been a violation of any Federal Trade Commission trade regulation rule, without regard to whether the credit repair organization—

(A) is engaged in commerce; or

(B) meets any other jurisdictional tests in the Federal Trade Commission Act.

(c) *State Action for Violations.*—

(1) *Authority of states.*—In addition to such other remedies as are provided under State law, whenever the chief law enforcement officer of a State, or an official or agency designated by a State, has reason to believe that any person has violated or is violating this title, the State—

(A) may bring an action to enjoin such violation;

(B) may bring an action on behalf of its residents to recover damages for which the person is liable to such residents under section 409 as a result of the violation; and

(C) in the case of any successful action under subparagraph (A) or (B), shall be awarded the costs of the action and reasonable attorney fees as determined by the court.

(2) *Rights of commission.*—

(A) *Notice to commission.*—The State shall serve prior written notice of any civil action under paragraph (1) upon the Federal Trade Commission and provide the Commission with a copy of its complaint, except in any case where such prior notice is not feasible, in which case the State shall serve such notice immediately upon instituting such action.

(B) *Intervention.*—The Commission shall have the right—

(i) to intervene in any action referred to in subparagraph (A);

(ii) upon so intervening, to be heard on all matters arising in the action; and

(iii) to file petitions for appeal.

(3) *Investigatory powers.*—For purposes of bringing any action under this subsection, nothing in this subsection shall prevent the chief law enforcement officer, or an official or agency designated by a State, from exercising the powers conferred on the chief law enforcement officer or such official by the laws of such State to conduct investigations or to administer oaths or affirmations or to compel the attendance of witnesses or the production of documentary and other evidence.

(4) *Limitation.*—Whenever the Federal Trade Commission has instituted a civil action for violation of this title, no State may, during the pen-

dency of such action, bring an action under this section against any defendant named in the complaint of the Commission for any violation of this title that is alleged in that complaint.

SEC. 411. STATUTE OF LIMITATIONS.

Any action to enforce any liability under this title may be brought before the later of —

(1) the end of the 5-year period beginning on the date of the occurrence of the violation involved; or

(2) in any case in which any credit repair organization has materially and willfully misrepresented any information which—

(A) the credit repair organization is required, by any provision of this title, to disclose to any consumer; and

(B) is material to the establishment of the credit repair organization's liability to the consumer under this title, the end of the 5-year period beginning on the date of the discovery by the consumer of the misrepresentation.

SEC. 412. RELATION TO STATE LAW.

This title shall not annul, alter, affect, or exempt any person subject to the provisions of this title from complying with any law of any State except to the extent that such law is inconsistent with any provision of this title, and then only to the extent of the inconsistency.

Appendix X

USING A LAWYER

When creditor negotiations are going nowhere, a lawyer can often get you the settlement you need. Once an attorney is involved, the creditor usually begins to worry about limiting liability. Most creditors are in business to make money, not to fight for the right to report derogatory credit.

Don't find your lawyer in the yellow pages. Call your Bar Association for a referral. Another good resource is the National Association of Consumer Advocates. Go to NACA.net, and use their "Find a Lawyer" tool to search for lawyers in your area. Make sure you narrow your search to lawyers who are "advanced" or "experienced" in the area of "credit reporting." You should realize that this is a search tool, not a referral, and that NACA has not necessarily vetted these lawyers.

Lawyers can be very expensive, so define the scope of your action and the pricing before working together. The consultation should be free.

A lawyer can:

- Define your strongest position in a dispute.
- Demand that the creditor prove it has met all its responsibilities (i.e., proper billing, notifications, and disclosures).
- Make affirmative arguments under, among other laws, the Fair Credit Reporting Act, the Fair Credit Billing Act, and Truth in Lending Act; as well as review the credit agreement and pursue lawsuits. These tactics put the creditor on the defensive.
- Negotiate an enforceable agreement that clears your credit in exchange for ending the dispute.